Praise for *Hidden Treasures*

"Have you ever gotten frustrated and agitated because you could not find something important to you, like a special treasure you wanted or needed badly? I have! I looked and searched until I was exhausted and sometimes gave up the search. That's the way it is until you find what you're looking for. Whether it's during times of peace and tranquility in life or times of sickness and pain, Robin has located what we are all looking for in this book. Find treasures that will inspire, motivate, encourage, and help you find the answers you need for your life of wholeness and peace."

—**Dr. Thelma Wells**, A Woman of God Ministries, television personality, professor, speaker, mentor, author

"When facing an illness or other life challenge, fear often stops the average person in their tracks—and becomes the biggest barrier to their hope and healing. Robin empowers readers with Bible-based tools on how to fight against the very thing that fights against them. From her personal experience, she gives practical tips for overcoming the inevitable moments of fear and discouragement. Hidden Treasures is a rich and valuable resource!"

—**Deborah Smith Pegues**, author of *30 Days to Taming Your Tongue*, CEO/founder of The Pegues Group, Inc.

"As we experience life, we at times face significant pain, pain that so often keeps us from realizing the many treasures within our lives. Our focus begins to revolve around these moments as if they were the predominant truths of our existence. *Hidden Treasures* is here to dispel the lie and help the reader unearth and discover what God has placed within: the treasure hidden in earthen vessels. So sit back, read, and follow a road map to finding all of your treasures, now."

—**Camy "Cameron" Arnett**, founder of Saving Destinies; producer/cohost *The Christian View*; CEO, Camy Arnett Production Studios

"'Our greatest treasures are often found in our greatest place of pain,' writes Robin Bertram. The author offers wisdom gained by walking through darkness and finding hope in the eternal God. Her Scripture-based insights will encourage families wrestling with questions in the midst of tragedy or caregivers helping a loved one navigate the journey toward heaven. *Hidden Treasures* is a faith-filled handbook overflowing with joy and hope."

—**Dianne Barker**, best-selling author, conference speaker, and host of "At the Library" on WHCB Radio, Johnson City, Tennessee

"Robin Bertram reminds the reader of just how important it is to be caring and compassionate during times of trial and pain with our words, actions, and intentions. It is a beautifully written resource full of valuable nuggets, share-worthy quotes, and a treasure chest overflowing with helpful tips."

—**Wendie Pett**, fitness and wellness expert, TV host of *Visibly Fit*, author, and speaker

"I stand in awe of Robin's honesty, determination, and courage as she faced her own personal health challenge. I stand in awe of her gentle voice as both writer and teacher. Hidden Treasures is merely an extension of her heart's desire to bring comfort, hope, and healing to those who are facing life's most difficult challenges. You will be blessed and encouraged as you read *Hidden Treasures*."

—**Jackie Carpenter**, host/executive producer of *The Christian View*, executive producer of the film *Stand Your Ground*, and author of *The Bridge* and *Georgia Justice*

"Compelling and captivating, *Hidden Treasures* offers hope through the truth of Scripture while families face some of their most difficult challenges. You will be encouraged and find great tools that will empower your loved one and your family. Robin reminds us that God is there. He is at work. He understands your pain."

—**Sue Detweiler**, author of *Women who Move Mountains*, speaker, radio host, and pastor of Life Bridge Church

"Robin Bertram is artfully transparent in sharing her own personal experiences in this book. *Hidden Treasures* is an invaluable, compassionate, and spiritual harvest of wise insights, which will both inspire and challenge the reader. This affirming message of hope and healing is a must read, a gem to be treasured."

—**Susan Mead**, author of *Dance with Jesus*

"In *Hidden Treasures* the reader will learn the importance of standing in faith, walking in faith, and fighting with faith. You will learn how to look beyond your circumstances and know that you are safe in God. You will learn that your faith can be a treasure God gives you. Robin has lived what she writes. I have been inspired as I read this book and I highly recommend it."

—**Sharon Hill**, author of the *OnCall Prayer Journal* and *The Power of Three*, coauthor of *The Most Powerful P Activity Book and Prayer Journal*

"*Hidden Treasures* is a jewel, a masterful work full of courage, honesty, and, above all, love. You will find valuable, practical methods, as well as day-to-day suggestions that are given to help ease the pain and to lighten the load of responsibility families face. But more than that, you will learn to see God at work in the midst of your pain; a wealth of wisdom!"

—**Deborah G. Ross**, Deborah Ross Ministries Inc., author of *Healing a Broken Marriage*, *Woman2Woman*, and *Save It!*

"Robin Bertram shares her heart and own personal experiences in this book. I was barely on page 2 before I was deeply touched. While reading, I was making a mental list of all the people I knew who desperately needed the treasures Robin has uncovered for us."

—**Deborah Dockery**, copastor of World Harvest Church North, coauthor of *The Invitation*

"Robin is gifted by the Lord as an exceptional author and teacher. Through her knowledge of God's Word and life experiences, she is able to reach people where they hurt. *Hidden Treasures* is an inspired work that stems from her own personal experiences with God in troubling times. Take a journey with Robin to find the 'hidden treasures' on your path to wholeness."

—Asa Dockery, author, columnist, and senior pastor at World Harvest Church North

"*Hidden Treasures* is a heartfelt, wise, honest, and tender book. It is enormously helpful both to those facing illness and to their loved ones. While there are many books on the subject of death and dying, few rely so deeply on the written Word of God to answer questions that seem to have no answer, and even fewer can offer a view through the lens of personal experience. This book offers practical solutions to the problems families must deal with when they are experiencing the degradation of one's quality of life or the potential loss of a loved one. A treasure waiting to be discovered!"

—**Suellen Roberts**, founder and president of the Christian Women in Media Association

"*Hidden Treasures* is expertly written by Robin Bertram. You will not want to stop reading the book until you finish it. It is a guide to find your own godly 'hidden treasures,' while also reading nuggets of Robin's personal life."

—**Patricia Mathis**, vice president of Community Television, Inc., WATC DT Atlanta

HIDDEN
TREASURES

FINDING HOPE AT THE
END OF LIFE'S JOURNEY

ROBIN BERTRAM

Abingdon Press
Nashville

HIDDEN TREASURES
FINDING HOPE AT THE END OF LIFE'S JOURNEY
Copyright © 2018 by Abingdon Press
All rights reserved.

Library of Congress Cataloging-in-Publication Data has been requested.

ISBN 978-1-5018-4546-8

Scripture quotations taken from the New American Standard Bible® (NASB), Copyright © 1960, 1962, 1963, 1968, 1971, 1972, 1973, 1975, 1977, 1995 by The Lockman Foundation. Used by permission. www.Lockman.org

Scripture quotations marked (ESV) are from the ESV Bible (The Holy Bible, English Standard Version®), copyright © 2001 by Crossway, a publishing ministry of Good News Publishers. Used by permission. All rights reserved.

Scripture quotations marked GW are taken from GOD'S WORD®, © 1995 God's Word to the Nations. Used by permission of Baker Publishing Group.

Scripture quotations marked KJV are from The Authorized (King James) Version. Rights in the Authorized Version in the United Kingdom are vested in the Crown. Reproduced by permission of the Crown's patentee, Cambridge University Press.

Quotations designated (NET) are from the NET Bible® copyright ©1996-2006 by Biblical Studies Press, L.L.C. http://netbible.com All rights reserved. Quoted by permission.

Scripture quotations marked (NIV) are taken from the Holy Bible, New International Version®, NIV®. Copyright © 1973, 1978, 1984, 2011 by Biblica, Inc.™ Used by permission of Zondervan. All rights reserved worldwide. www.zondervan.com The "NIV" and "New International Version" are trademarks registered in the United States Patent and Trademark Office by Biblica, Inc.™

Scripture quotations marked NKJV are taken from the New King James Version®. Copyright © 1982 by Thomas Nelson. Used by permission. All rights reserved.

Scripture quotations marked NLT are taken from the Holy Bible, New Living Translation, copyright ©1996, 2004, 2015 by Tyndale House Foundation. Used by permission of Tyndale House Publishers, Inc., Carol Stream, Illinois 60188. All rights reserved.

Scripture quotations marked NLV are taken from the New Life Version copyright © 1969 and 2003. Used by permission of Barbour Publishing, Inc., Uhrichsville, Ohio, 44683. All rights reserved.

Scripture quotations marked NRSV are taken from the New Revised Standard Version Bible, copyright © 1989 National Council of the Churches of Christ in the United States of America. Used by permission. All rights reserved worldwide. http://nrsvbibles.org/

Scripture quotations marked WEB are taken from the World English Bible. Public domain.

18 19 20 21 22 23 24 25 26—10 9 8 7 6 5 4 3 2 1
MANUFACTURED IN THE UNITED STATES OF AMERICA

CONTENTS

CONTENTS

So Jesus said to them, "The Light is among you for a little while longer. Walk while you have the light, lest darkness overtake you. The one who walks in the darkness does not know where he is going. While you have the light, believe in the light, that you may become sons of light."

—*John 12:35-36 ESV*

PREFACE

My dear father was given a death sentence thirty years before he died. I watched him live with dignity and I watched him die with dignity. He lay on his deathbed and said to me, "Robin, I have no regrets." What a way to live! It took me several years after his death to understand such a statement, but after sitting at the bedside of numerous sick and dying individuals, it became very apparent to me what he actually meant.

Many people are facing life-threatening diseases, terminal illness, and the long-term care of elderly parents but have few resources to rely on in such difficult and challenging times. They strive to keep their challenges private and end up suffering in silence with no real support system. *Hidden Treasures* will become an important resource for them because it provides sound advice based on both Scripture and personal experience.

Though there are many books on the subject of death and dying, few rely as heavily as this book on the written Word of God to answer questions that seem to have no answer, and even fewer can offer a view through the lens of personal experience. This book offers practical solutions to the problems families must deal with when they are experiencing the degradation of the quality of their life or the potential loss of a loved one.

Hidden Treasures will inspire, motivate, and encourage families to begin to walk the road to heaven without the fear and anxiety associated with this challenging time. Through the personal case studies utilized in the book, readers will find comfort as they begin to view their situation from a heavenly perspective. How? Through the truth found in the Scriptures combined with the insight gained from real-life stories with victorious outcomes.

Hidden Treasures also offers tools that will aid an individual and family to take charge of their situation, become victors instead of victims, and enjoy the beauty that surrounds them as they begin to gaze on the treasures at heaven's gates.

There are very few things that are certain and predictable in life, things that are common to all and that each of us must encounter. We will all face death at some point, and many of us will also be faced with some form of pain and suffering along the way. It may be related to our own experience or could be that of a dear loved one.

Despite the inevitability and universality of suffering and death, there is tremendous diversity in how we approach the challenges we face. Some charge ahead and "take control," others look to surround themselves with a team for support and solace, and still others strive to keep their challenges private, suffering in silence with no real support system. Beyond these outward approaches to how we might face suffering and death, there is also a broad range of emotions experienced, from rock-solid, faithful confidence to trembling fear and anxiety.

During twenty-five years of prayer ministry, I have had the

honor and privilege of ministering to numerous people facing dire life challenges. A few years ago, I was also faced with my own life-altering, life-threatening diagnosis, giving me a clearer picture of the thoughts, concerns, and emotions that arise when faced with death. In some cases the outcome was victorious healing and restoration, while in others it was the sorrowful release of a loved one to the Lord. Yet, in each and every situation, regardless of the outcome, we were able to clearly witness God at work: in the person who was ill, in their family members, and even in the surrounding community as they witnessed the powerful faith being exhibited. May you be comforted and encouraged as you join along with me in this journey.

The fear of death follows from the fear of life. A man who lives fully is prepared to die at any time.

—Mark Twain

Introduction

Several years ago I sat at the bedside of my dying friend Jack. He had decided on funeral arrangements and asked if I would preach his funeral. He proceeded to tell me how he wanted things handled. You see, my friend managed his life well . . . and he managed his death equally as well. I asked him, "Jack, what do you want me to say?" He gave me three distinct messages he wanted me to share. The first thing he told me was, "Tell them the truth." We laughed. That would be very easy to do. I knew what he meant. Jack was known for telling you how he felt about things. You always knew where he stood on an issue, and I loved Jack for that. He never tried to be politically correct, and he really didn't care how you felt about his opinions. He encouraged me, saying, "Just say what you mean, and mean what you say. There is safety in truth." He would also emphatically state, "If you tell the truth, you only have to say it once, so tell them the truth."

I loved Jack's heart and attitude. Jack didn't care if he ruffled feathers; truth was important to him. Even in the planning of his funeral, he spoke of his internal beliefs. His faith had legs. His personal religious ideals were more than simply a conceptual way of thinking, but for him it was a way of life.

Jack, an older man in his midsixties, had only been retired a few years when a vicious form of carcinoma got the best of him. He taught me a lot during his six-year struggle. I was blessed to walk beside him as he faced this terrible disease, and it was through that time that I witnessed tremendous strength, courage, and faith. I learned a lot about the process of living and dying. He chose to stand on the written Word of God for most of his life and certainly during the process of his death. He was a man of great courage, and the truth of God's Word gave him that courage.

Have you ever wondered how people can face death and know that their days are limited? It seems to me that a quick death would be more gracious. I often felt that a fast track out was easier for everyone to deal with. How can individuals face death with courage and peace? How do families get through it? Where can they find the inner strength to face each day, knowing that there will come a time when their precious loved one will no longer be with them? I learned many answers to these questions through my experience with Jack. My life will never be the same.

Every individual who faces long-term or terminal illness will have times of deep introspection and questioning, and most will struggle with bouts of fear, anger, and depression. They may even be angry with God. What you think or believe can greatly impact your journey, and a firm foundation will definitely ease the discomfort of the unknown. If you died today, would you know for certain that you would spend eternity in heaven? If you took your last breath, do you really believe that you will still exist? Or do you believe that you will simply come to an end?

The time will come when each of us will face death. Most people have someone who is currently dealing with a physical illness or an elderly family member nearing the end of life. When facing the realization that tomorrow may not come, all must come face to face with their deepest, most personal beliefs like no other time in their life's journey.

I assure you, I understand your pain. I understand the pain of watching a loved one's health slowly deteriorate. I understand the pain of watching a small child have to let go of his mother's hand when he crosses over to be with Jesus. I understand the grief a father feels when he leaves a loving wife and young children behind. I understand the pain of an elderly man who lives his last days trying to prove his love to an alienated loved one.

The purpose for writing this book is so you, too, will know what it means to live well and to die well. I am writing this book for those who need and want to be comforted, for families who must cope with difficult situations when a loved one is sick, and to share the wisdom gained from many who have faced the unknown with peace, joy, and even acceptance.

The principles in this book will bring great comfort and practical tools for families who are taking care of an elderly family member, those whose loved one is facing long-term illness, or those who are terminally ill. As you read this book, you will gain understanding of how to approach those who are facing long-term or terminal illness and their families and to bring comfort to them during their time of struggle. You will have a better picture of heaven as you read the personal accounts of those facing death. You will learn how to face your own fears with dignity.

Within this book you will find:

- **Nuggets of Wisdom:** These are specific Scriptures that have given me comfort, wisdom, and insight during my personal journey. I believe they will do the same for you.
- **Treasure Chest:** At the end of each chapter, there are seven key principles that will help you find light in the midst of your darkness and will encourage you to be strong, knowing that God is sending blessings and treasured moments all along the way.
- **Shareworthy:** There are text boxes scattered throughout each chapter that include quotes expanding on the ideas in this book and that I hope you will consider sharing on your social media platforms.
- **Love in Action:** This is sound advice and practical suggestions for families who are facing real-life struggles of long-term illnesses.

I certainly don't know the circumstances you are facing today. You may have just received word that you have a life-threatening illness, you may be caring for a parent who is approaching their final days, or you may be the parent of a sick child. Regardless of the circumstance, this I know: God knows, God sees, and God cares.

My prayer as you read this book is that you will be encouraged in the midst of your challenges and that you will achieve a level of "faithful expectancy" knowing that God is with you and is working miracles, hidden treasures, all around you. May God strengthen and encourage you as we walk through this journey together.

Grace and peace to you,
Robin

PART ONE

LOOKING INWARD

Open now thy gates of beauty,
Zion, let me enter there,
Where my soul in joyful duty
Waits for God who answers prayer.
Oh, how blessed is this place,
Filled with solace, light, and grace!

—Benjamin Schmolck,
"Open Now Thy Gates of Beauty"

CHAPTER 1

TREASURES

It was 2 a.m.

Earlier that night, several other ministers and I were called to the home of a sweet little girl who battled severe heart disease. I had walked with this family for several years while in the midst of their own personal darkness. They became my family, and this little girl, Ava, not yet ten years old, was like one of my own. We knew her time was short. We prayed. We fasted. We believed she would get better, yet we stood with this little child at the gates of heaven.

Ava had long, curly blonde hair and big blue eyes—the kind of eyes that would melt your very soul. She was cheerful and bubbly on her good days, and, although her body was weak, her spirit was strong. She was the type of child who wanted everybody she knew to go to heaven. She would often ask me about people we knew—friends and neighbors—"Do you think they really know Jesus, Miss Robin? We need to tell them about Him."

I was a regular in Ava's home. She would call me night or day, and I would drop everything and go to her. I believed that God was going to heal this little one, even until the very moment she took her last breath. We were all there that night: her mom, dad, two other friends, and me. It had been our ritual, night after night, to stop by Ava's home, gather around her bed, and pray. That night was no different, except it would be our last.

SHAREWORTHY

They that love beyond the world cannot be separated by it. Death cannot kill what never dies.

—*William Penn*

That night, before her death, Ava went around the room and said, "I love you, Miss Robin. I love you, Miss Melanie. I love you, Pastor John. I love you, Momma. I love you, Daddy. I love you, Jesus." This, too, was Ava's nightly ritual. But now, Ava's breathing had become intensely laborious. With bated breath, we watched every inhale and exhale. Her little body couldn't take much more. The hospice nurse had left, reluctantly, knowing that it was just a matter of time. Mom and Dad wanted privacy with their sweet, little child but had asked the prayer ministers to stay. As we cried out to Jesus, one of the prayer ministers noticed Ava's body getting warm; one last glimmer of hope, at least we thought. Ava was somewhat lucid and asked her momma if she could go with her. Ava's mom told her she could not, but that Jesus would be there with her when she left. He was.

Gates of Heaven

As Ava took her last breath, her mom fell out cold; her body stretched out over her little girl's body. We could not wake her for several moments. I've often wondered if God let her walk with Ava to the gates of heaven. Of course, there is no biblical basis for that, just a sweet thought in my own mind, because I know how kind and loving God is. I know that when you close your eyes here on earth, you will open them there in the presence of Jesus. When Ava's mom came to, Ava was gone. At that very moment, I fell off the bed and onto the floor. My face was plunged into the carpet, silent. I could hardly breathe. The tangible presence of God was so overwhelming to me that I knew I could not get up off the floor. It was weighty. It was holy. It was undeniable. God's glory fell, and in that moment, I experienced the infinite perfections of His grace and mercy. Love covered us like a blanket—the entire room and everyone in it. No one said a word. It was just penetratingly silent. He had come for one of His own, and of that I am sure.

NUGGETS OF WISDOM: Precious in the sight of the LORD is the death of his saints.

(Psalm 116:15 KJV)

As I look back at that tremendous experience, several things come to mind. God does not leave us on our own but, instead, is there to walk with us through our own personal darkness. He is always working behind the scenes. His power and His love are tangible, and His plans will go forth. That night, I learned a lot about life and death. I learned about faith and fear. I learned that a walk with God is a walk in the light, even when we are in the midst of utter darkness.

SHAREWORTHY

God's imminent power shows up at the very
moment of our impending misfortune.
—Robin Bertram

The Gold Box

While my family visited my husband's brother and his family,
we sat in the kitchen reminiscing about the past, with some especially fond remembrances of my husband's favorite aunt, Virginia,
who had recently passed. Though married and a retired professional
at the time of her death, she had been a nun for most of her adult
life. She was a quiet, humble woman who lived in a small townhome
near the outer suburbs of Philadelphia. She was not a flashy person
in her appearance but rather plain and simple, certainly a no-bling
kind of lady.

My mother-in-law requested that she speak with me privately.
While standing in the back bedroom, she reached into her purse,
pulled out a lovely gold box, and placed it in my hand. "This is for
you," she said. I opened it, and inside was a beautifully jeweled
slide bracelet with twenty-one precious and semiprecious stones.
The box contained a slip of paper with my name handwritten on it
from dear Aunt Virginia. That incredibly thoughtful gift was meant
especially for me. As tears streamed down my face, I became overwhelmed with a sense of love and joy, not because of the actual value
of the gemstones, but because of the spirit behind the gift. The fact
that she had taken the time to personally write my name on this gift
and assign it to me, long before she knew she would be leaving this

world, was astounding. This bracelet was one of her most treasured possessions, and she so graciously decided to leave it for me.

SHAREWORTHY

God will turn blight into blessing, trauma into treasures, and bring healing out of hurt. Watch for His hand. He is always at work.

—*Robin Bertram*

Several years ago, I faced my own mortality. Little did I know at the time that I would be given a death sentence with no chance of recovery. My doctors shared the possibility of four dire diseases, subsequently took three off the table, and left the worst scenario. I was told that the disease I potentially had would kill me within two years. There was no cure and there was no treatment. For one year, I waited to die. It was during this first year that I had to deal with many internal struggles related to the importance of life and the importance of death. Several questions continually came to mind: *Am I significant? Has my life had any real value? Have I accomplished all the Lord has asked of me? How am I going to get through this?* I realized that I had more questions than answers. I began to look fervently at the lessons I had gleaned from past experiences with others who had gone through tragedy or life-challenging situations. What did I really believe? I had to start in my own heart.

NUGGETS OF WISDOM: Do not store up for yourselves treasures on earth, where moth and rust destroy, and where thieves break in and steal. But store up for yourselves treasures in heaven, where neither moth nor rust destroys, and where thieves do not break in and steal; for where your treasure is, there your heart will be also. (Matthew 6:19-21)

Treasures of Heavenly Value

I began to look inward. So let's start this journey together by looking for those treasures that are hidden inside. This is a time when you will go through serious introspection. Each of us has treasures that have been locked away inside, and we just have to discover them so that they can be adequately shared with others.

Let's first understand some principles regarding treasures: Treasures are often concealed in the dark, they are usually hidden from plain view, they must be mined or sought after, and they often reflect light or are made of a highly reflective material. Rarely are they displayed out in the open. Treasures are accessed by those willing to work for them and those willing to pay the price to seek after them. It takes time to unearth hidden treasures. It takes time, patience, and a desire.

When you understand who you are in Christ and what is truly inside of you, you will be able to handle the trials, struggles, and difficulties that may be ahead of you. Whatever your journey might be right now, be well aware that God has hidden treasures all along the way. We just have to see them and have a desire to find them. Jesus commanded His disciples to not lay up treasures on earth, which would just rot away, but rather to lay up treasures in heaven. So, if true treasures are not found in earthly possessions, where are they found?

Seven Keys to Unlocking Hidden Treasures

How do we find what is hidden within? Let's look into our treasure chest, the Word of God, to guide us. It is the most valuable source to discover real eternal treasures. Think with me about the story of Ruth found in the Bible. The Book of Ruth was written during the period of Judges, possibly between 1350 BC and 1100 BC. The land of Judah was in a time of spiritual confusion and compromise, and apostasy was the word of the day. From this setting, there is a message for us today that pertains to God's sufficiency, His grace, His mercy, and our ability to see Him at work in the midst of our trials.

What starts out to be a story of pain, loss, famine, death, and despair, quickly becomes a story of protection, provision, redemption, and restoration. The characters are exemplary in portraying the depth of loyalty, commitment, and servanthood that should mirror the life and walk of every dedicated believer. Naomi lost her husband and two sons and became so bitter that she changed her name from Naomi, which means "pleasant, delightful," to Mara, which means "bitter." Throughout the story, Naomi struggled to see God at work, but He was. Ruth, her daughter-in-law, returned with her to her homeland, was discovered by a rich nobleman named Boaz, ultimately marrying him and giving Naomi a grandson that she thought she would never have. The child that was born was in the lineage of King David, ultimately leading to Jesus. God had the big picture.

NUGGETS OF WISDOM: Where you go, I will go; and where you stay, I will stay. Your people will be my people, and your God my God. (Ruth 1:16 WEB)

Looking at Ruth's life, we see that she was widowed, poor, and struggling, yet she found her treasure working in a corner of a field, which had been reserved for those in great poverty. Had she not been willing to go with Naomi and work in the field, she would have missed Boaz, one of her greatest treasures.

I want to share with you some keys that I devised to help others find the treasures hidden within them.

Key #1: To find the treasures within takes work, dedication, and loyalty to the cause at hand, regardless of your circumstances.

Ruth was a poor young widow who was determined to stay with her mother-in-law through thick and thin. They had no future, as far as they could see, but in reality, they did. Naomi's wisdom and guidance helped Ruth find the new home she so desperately desired and the new family to fulfill her life. *Naomi thought she had nothing to give.*

Do you remember the account of Esther found in the Bible? Esther was a beautiful young peasant girl from humble beginnings, orphaned by the death of both parents, raised by her uncle, Mordecai, and called to change the fate of a nation. Her courage and passion resounded in her willingness and obedience to lay down her life for the sake of her people. Her life had purpose. Esther had a hidden treasure, but she had to dig deep for it to be brought out in the fullness of time.

What is stored deeply in your soul?

Are there decisions that can be made now that will determine the fate of your own family?

One of Esther's hidden treasures was her Jewish roots, a secret that could have cost Esther her life had it been known by others. Esther, through the process of her training under Mordecai, gained knowledge and understanding of what was really important. Esther knew it was not her position or beauty. She knew it was not the luxury of the king's palace. She knew it was not the honor due her. Esther knew the most important thing was the salvation of God's people. She was willing to risk her own life to save the lives of the people she loved. What was at risk was the annihilation of an entire nation, the destruction of God's chosen people ... His treasured possessions.

Key #2: Value God and what He values.

Do you know what God values? Have you aligned your desires with His desires? Esther had to make an exchange. Her hidden Jewish identity had to be exposed, even at the potential of losing her life, so that her godly identity could come into being. The divine destiny of God relied upon Esther's understanding of her own hidden treasures.

Do you see yourself as God sees you? Do you know your true identity in Christ?

Key #3: Every eternal treasure found will require sacrifice.

Abraham, the father of nations, found his treasure in sacrifice. Abraham entered into a covenant with God. God said to Abraham, "As for Me, behold, My covenant with you, And you will be the father of a multitude of nations" (Genesis 17:4). An everlasting covenant was established that could not be broken. It was not reliant on man. It was a divine agreement that would be perpetually acknowledged because it was grounded solely in the sovereign will of God. However, there would be a cost, and the price was high. Read the full account in Genesis 22:9-19. Had Abraham not been willing to sacrifice his very dream, his own blood, his future, he would not have inherited nations. The promised inheritance came through his children. He had to let go and sacrifice his own dream to obtain God's best, God's plan for him, and God's direction. Abraham knew the voice of God. Abraham knew God as his sure foundation. He knew God as the God who would provide.

> NUGGETS OF WISDOM: He said, "Do not stretch out your hand against the lad, and do nothing to him; for now I know that you fear God, since you have not withheld your son, your only son, from Me." (Genesis 22:12)

Are you holding on to something that you must let go? Are you holding on to your future as if it were in your control? Is it time to lay your most treasured possessions—your dreams, your plans, and your goals—on the altar of sacrifice? Hard to do, I know, but there are eternal treasures that await you when you lay down your plans and follow after God's plan.

Key #4: God is our sure foundation, and obedience and the fear of the Lord are essential.

Every great hero, man or woman of faith, moved under the direction of God, even when things did not make sense in the natural. Every one of them obeyed, even if it meant the sacrifice of their life or the lives of their loved ones. Every great man or woman of God recognized God's voice and chose to follow, even if it meant separation from the treasures they so deservedly had in store.

> NUGGETS OF WISDOM: There will be stability in your times, abundance of salvation, wisdom, and

knowledge. The fear of Yahweh is your treasure. (Isaiah 33:6 WEB)

When going through hardships, you need God's grace and mercy to get you through. You need the comfort of His Spirit. You need the strength of His love. You need the gift of His forgiveness. Is He your strong foundation? Have you found your true identity in Him?

NUGGETS OF WISDOM: If you cry out to know right from wrong, and lift your voice for understanding; if you look for her as silver, and look for her as hidden riches; then you will understand the fear of the Lord, and find what is known of God. (Proverbs 2:3-5 NLV)

Key # 5: You will have to give up what is rightly yours to obtain what the Lord has in store for your future.

Jesus gave up worldly rule to gain eternal rule. Esther gave up her natural birthright to find her spiritual birthright. Abraham gave up his only son to gain sons of all nations. Now, let's look at what Moses had to give up. The Bible says, "Then Pharaoh gave this order to all his people: 'Every boy that is born you must throw into the Nile, but let every girl live'" (Exodus 1:22 NIV). The Bible tells us that Moses was no ordinary child. His mother saw him as a fine boy because she recognized the greatness within him. She hid him in a basket—a treasure waiting to be found. Pharaoh's daughter took him as her own child. He was educated in the wisdom of the Egyptians and, according to Acts 7:22, was powerful in speech and action. His future was dependent on someone finding the hidden treasure, but Moses would have to find his own treasures hidden within.

> NUGGETS OF WISDOM: Then she put the child into it and set it among the reeds by the bank of the Nile. His sister stood at a distance to find out what would happen to him. (Exodus 2:3-4)

What were those treasures hidden within Moses? Why was he so special? What made God decide to choose him to be the greatest deliverer of all times? What did Moses have to give up to find his hidden treasures? Moses gave up all the riches of Pharaoh.

There was a point of decision, a point in time, when Moses chose to look forward to his spiritual rewards, leaving behind what was rightfully his while exchanging his natural inheritance for his spiritual inheritance. Not only did Moses give up great possessions, but he also determined to walk faithfully forward with God.

> NUGGETS OF WISDOM: He chose to be mistreated along with the people of God rather than to enjoy the pleasures of sin for a short time. He regarded disgrace for the sake of Christ as of greater value than the treasures of Egypt, because he was looking ahead to his reward.
> (Hebrews 11:25-26 NIV)

Key #6: You must walk faithfully with the Lord to find your own treasures within.

Let the Lord show you the inner treasures. The Lord will show you things you never knew about yourself. He will give you strength. He will encourage you along the way if you take the time to see them. He will show you the treasures you have inside, as well as the treasured moments and signs that you would have normally passed right on by.

Let's examine our last key.

Key #7: Our greatest treasures are often found in our greatest place of pain.

We are reminded of this truth when Jesus was in the garden of Gethsemane.

We are reminded of this truth through the historical accounts of the men and women of God identified above.

These saints of God found their treasures:

- Abraham, as he raised the knife to slay his only son.
- Esther, at the point of decision, "If I perish, I perish" (Esther 4:16).
- Moses, as he left the riches of the house of Pharaoh.

Each of us has a treasure trove stored inside. Each has a golden box full of real treasures. Each of us is reflective of God's light even in our deepest pain. It's time to unearth those hidden treasures.

God Moments

Years ago, before my father went to be with Jesus, he told me that he wanted me to have his accordion. I had never played the accordion, nor do I intend to do so, but I knew that my father loved that accordion. It was a Silvertone C-20, made in Italy. The bellows-driven and free-reed aerophone-type, colloquially referred to as a squeezebox. The body was mother-of-pearl, and the keyboard had ivory and satin ebony keys. I was so elated. I remember many nights sitting in my living room with my dad singing old gospel hymns as he played that beautiful instrument. Every Friday night we would prepare for Sunday service, and Dad would gather us and pull out his handwritten songbook. That accordion, despite being old and beautiful, didn't have much monetary value. Its worth was reflected in the sentiment of having something that my dad had loved so dearly. It was an extension of my father's love and, to this day, represents a tremendous gift passed forward, as well as the treasure of heartfelt moments spent with my dad when I was growing up. Something money can't buy.

Looking Inward

God is sovereign, and He is moving in and through your circumstances. He will move for your good and for His glory. No matter your struggle right now, trust that God will not leave you and He will not forsake you. Even in the midst of your darkness and your pain, He will bring treasures along the way.

As I stood with her at the gates of heaven, Ava taught me great lessons about life and death that I treasure. For me, the handwritten note attached to the gold box was a beautiful message of love from Aunt Virginia. And as far as my father goes, it was the song in his heart that molded and shaped my destiny through his faithfulness to God.

My prayer is, through this book, you will see God at work in many ways to show Himself to you, to show the love He has for you, and to show you many treasures He has prepared all along the way.

Know God. Find yourself.

Know God's voice. Find your treasures.

Know God's heart. Find your passions.

Know God's plan. Find your purpose in life and in death.

TREASURE CHEST

- To find the treasures within takes work, dedication, and loyalty to the cause at hand, regardless of your circumstances.

- Value God and what He values, and you yourself will be valued.

- Every treasure found of eternal value requires sacrifice.

- God is our sure foundation, and obedience and the fear of the Lord are the key.

- You will have to give up what is rightly yours to obtain what the Lord has in store for your future.

- You must walk faithfully and fearlessly with the Lord to find your own treasures within.

- Our greatest treasures are often found in our greatest place of pain.

How firm a foundation, ye saints of the Lord,
Is laid for your faith in His excellent Word!
What more can He say than to you He hath said
Who unto the Savior for refuge have fled? . . .
When through fiery trials thy pathway shall lie,
My grace, all-sufficient, shall be thy supply.
The flames shall not hurt thee; I only design
Thy dross to consume and thy gold to refine.

—Robert Keen, *"How Firm a Foundation,*
Ye Saints of the Lord"

CHAPTER 2

FIRM FOUNDATION

My story begins with my own potential diagnosis, which would guarantee inevitable death, with no treatment available, and an immensely long and painful path to the grave. I was given four potential diagnoses, three of which offered some form of treatment for prolonging my life while the fourth had none available. Mayo Clinic took the first three off the table and left me with the last potential diagnosis. They said, "There is no cure, and there is no treatment available." I went home and waited for the symptoms to worsen, and I prepared to die. During that time, I wrote my living will. I made decisions regarding my funeral. I put things in order. But first, let's jump back to the real beginning of my story some twenty years ago when God was teaching me things about Himself that I did not clearly understand.

> NUGGETS OF WISDOM: And the world is passing away, and the lust of it; but he who does the will of God abides forever. (1 John 2:17 NKJV)

Faulty Foundations

When we were first married, my husband, Ken, and I used to love to look at homes that were under construction or going up for sale. I was always amazed at how a home would take shape. First the foundation was laid, then the shell of the house with the studs, the roof would go on, then walls would go up. I loved watching the different phases of the construction, something beautiful being formed with each new phase.

One day we decided to go look at a house that was for sale. It was a massive house for an unexpectedly low price. I could not believe what I was looking at. The home was in a small town in Virginia. We decided to take the two-hour drive because this house would be a steal if it were truly as it was listed in the real estate magazine. The house sat upon a hill in a nice golf course community. Parts of the roof were made out of copper. It had large, beautiful windows that overlooked the valley. I was so excited. We thought we had found a gold mine.

We met the Realtor at the front door, and she seemed to be as excited about the house as we were. We walked from one spacious room to the next. The kitchen had granite countertops, great appliances, beautiful tile, and hardwood flooring throughout the home. It could not have been prettier. Then I noticed some spots on the wall—black spots. Then I noticed some cracks around the windowsills. The more we looked, the more we saw.

"What is this?" I asked.

The Realtor explained that when the home was built there had been difficulties with the foundation. It had been improperly constructed. The house was ruined due to a faulty foundation, which did not provide the security necessary to hold the house up. Cracks, black mold, and water damage destroyed the home from the foundation up. Renovation costs alone would be astronomical. My heart sank.

As I pulled away, God began to teach me about the importance of a good foundation. He impressed upon me the importance of building a home, a marriage, or a family on a strong, biblical foundation because the storms of life would come, and only that which was built on a good foundation would stand through it all. Your faith is the same way. It has to be built upon a good foundation. If not, when the storms do come, it will be destroyed.

Perhaps that is your struggle now. Do you have faith? What has it been built on? Do you believe in an all-powerful, all-knowing, and ever-present God who loves you and who will be with you on your life's journey? Build your foundation on the truth of who Jesus is and what He has already done for you. Jesus is our firm foundation.

NUGGETS OF WISDOM: But the one who has heard and has not acted accordingly, is like a man who built a house on the ground without any foundation; and the torrent burst against it and immediately it collapsed, and the ruin of that house was great. (Luke 6:49)

Jesus Christ, as He hung on the cross, stated emphatically to the thief hanging by His side, "Today you shall be with Me in Paradise" (Luke 23:43). Have you ever wondered what will happen when you have to leave this world? Perhaps you have a friend or loved one who is facing this very possibility. Maybe you are. Comfort comes to all regardless of the circumstance, when they first settle in their hearts a sure belief in, and a decision to accept fully, with childlike faith, the words of the Holy Bible. It offers comfort. It offers answers. It offers hope. It is the truth we stand on.

Herein lies the importance of a personal belief system. What you think or believe can greatly impact the journey. Would you be able to handle the long days ahead? Would you be able to handle dark, hard, difficult times of internal struggle? A firm foundation will definitively ease the discomfort of the unknown. If you died today, would you know for certain that you would spend eternity in heaven? If you took your last breath, do you really believe that you would still exist, that your spirit is eternal? Or do you believe that you would simply come to an abrupt end? Is there life after death? Do you believe there is a heaven? If so, what would it be like?

Life Eternal

In the Gospel of John, we read that when an individual dies, he actually enters life. I clearly remember reading in Ezekiel that the righteous will never die (18:21-22). I thought to myself, *We all die, but I know the Bible is true. How then can this Scripture tell me something I know to be incorrect? What does this mean?* Perhaps you've had the same question. We will all die. Our bodies will decay. We will all come to an end here on this earth. We will all leave family and loved ones one day. I had questions as I read this passage in the Bible that spoke of the hereafter. *What actually happens to you when you die?*

It was the same question I struggled with when I tried to understand the term *born again*. What does this term really mean? Have you pondered the term or the process? To understand life after death, one must first understand being born again from above.

NUGGETS OF WISDOM: It is the Spirit who gives
life; the flesh profits nothing. (John 6:63)

If you've ever visited a funeral home, you can see the relevance in
this statement. Our flesh is useless when we die. It is empty, devoid
of spirit, though man's spirit is eternal. We can be like a dead man
walking before salvation. We have no understanding of the eternal
life that we can have. God breathes on us and we are born again—
not by water but by the Spirit. The breath of God brings rebirth,
redemption, and reconciliation. He breathes life into our deadness.
We are, in essence, born into the family of God when we acknowledge and confess the birth, death, burial, and resurrection of Jesus
Christ. This occurs when we believe in our heart and confess with
our mouth that Jesus Christ is Lord. We choose to follow God. We
also decide to turn away from our sinful ways. It is at this point in
time that we actually gain victory over death. Yes, I did say victory.
It is at this point in time when we become spiritual beings with a
promise of life everlasting.

Resurrection Power

Pain and sorrow in this lifetime are to be expected; trials, tribulation, sickness, and death are inevitable. Eventually, we all will face
death. Although inevitable, death is a part of our existence that we
really do not understand. However, the apostle Paul instructs us in
the Bible that death is a subject about which we cannot afford to be
ignorant. We need hope that is built on a solid foundation. There are
things we can know for certain. We do know that to be absent in the
body is to be present with the Lord (see 2 Corinthians 5:8). We do
know that we cannot put on the imperishable until we take off the

perishable (see 1 Corinthians 15:53). We do know that this earthly body is but a tent of clay and that our spirit and soul will be united with Christ when we leave this world and pass over into eternity. How do we know? Because it is written in God's Word, and God cannot lie. In this we build our strong foundation so that we will not be moved in the time of struggle or difficulty.

> NUGGETS OF WISDOM: Jesus said to her, "I am the resurrection and the life. Those who believe in me, even though they die, will live."
> (John 11:25 NRSV)

As life hits us with difficulty, we can react in many ways. Our reactions are formed based on our core beliefs. God gave us a perfect road map as we journey through uncharted waters. Trials, tribulations, sickness, and death are inevitable, but how we deal with the possibilities can determine how we spend the time we have left on earth. If you or a loved one is facing such difficulty, wouldn't you want to be certain that God has all the answers you need, all the comfort you cry out for, and all the promises upon which you will need to stand? He does, and it is written. Delve into the Word of God with me and be strengthened.

> NUGGETS OF WISDOM: "Lord, behold, he whom You love is sick." But when Jesus heard this, He said, "This sickness is not to end in death, but for the glory of God, so that the Son of God may be glorified by it." (John 11:3-4)

Helped by God

The eleventh chapter of the Gospel of John offers a wonderful picture of the resurrection power of Christ. It is an account of a man named Lazarus who was sick and died. His name means "God has helped." This account, one of Jesus' greatest miracles, gives us a level of security like no other account recorded in history, and through it we begin to understand resurrection power. Through the story of Lazarus, we understand the power of our living Savior to not just raise the dead or call our bodies out of the grave at the rapture, but to deal with our here and now, to deal with real-life issues today.

As we look at this biblical account, we begin to understand that God cares about our smallest needs, that He truly hears our cries, and that He desires to comfort and strengthen us through our trials. You may remember the story. Jesus gets word that one of his dearest friends, Lazarus, is sick. Instead of immediately rushing to his side, He waits two days where He is.

We do not understand God's ways or His timing, but here is a critical lesson: God's timing is not always our timing. After the delay, Jesus journeys back to Bethany, a city where they had previously tried to stone Him. The disciples go with Jesus, thinking they are on the way to their own demise. When He arrives, Martha says, "Lord, if You had been here, my brother would not have died" (John 11:21).

Can God restore?

We are going to look at restoration and resurrection and see from this account what we can learn. You might be thinking, *It's too late. I've been told there is nothing they can do.* God gives life. He is the restorer of dead things.

Get this now. Lazarus was not asleep. He was not in a coma. He was not in a catatonic state of being. He was dead—just plain dead (see John 11:14).

Why is this account so incredibly important? Because you cannot understand the power of an omnipresent God who is truly omnipotent until you first understand that this man was DEAD. He was physically dead, with no breath in his body. He was wrapped in a tomb for four consecutive days. Can God breathe His breath upon a dead thing and have it come back to life again?

One of the clearest examples of resurrection power is here, right here, right now. It is right inside of you, if you have truly been born again. That old man is dead, and a new creature in Christ has risen: the greatest treasure we can ever find in life. Have you found it?

Salvation is the restorative power of Christ flowing through you so you become a new creature in Christ. We have a Father in heaven who is all-powerful. Nothing is impossible for those who believe.

SHAREWORTHY

He restores the spirit. He restores the soul.
He can restore the body.
—*Robin Bertram*

NUGGETS OF WISDOM: Jesus replied, "Very truly I tell you, no one can see the kingdom of God unless they are born again." (John 3:3 NIV)

Jesus was handed over to death for our sins and was raised to life for our justification. That's resurrection power. That's omnipotence.

What do I mean by omnipotent? I mean God is all-powerful, therefore able to do anything. God exercises His power according to His purposes.

Let me repeat myself. God exercises His power according to His purposes. There is nothing too big for God. There are no different levels of difficulty. He spoke the world into existence. Can anything be too hard for Him?

If Only

Back to our story ... Mary said, "But Jesus, he is dead." *But Jesus, if only You had been there. If only.* You can hear the pain ring through her words. You can hear her anguish. You can hear the disappointment. *If only ... But Jesus ... If only.*

What is your *If only*?

Ask yourself.

Martha confidently ran out and met Jesus as He approached. Mary stayed behind with no hope at all. Mary was the one who had anointed His feet with her tears. She was the one who rested at Jesus' feet. She was the one who intently listened to His words. Would she rest in the midst of her own trial, her own crisis? Is her staying behind a sign of defeat or faithful assurance? I ask you, was she resting or had she given up in deep anguish?

What About You

Where are you today? Do you know that Jesus is there with you? Do you know that Jesus cares about you? Do you know that He knows what you are going through? Do you know He hears you? Do you know that Jesus loves you deeply?

Perhaps you do not feel very loved right now. I understand, believe me. But remember, Jesus gave His life so that you could have life. That's how much He cares for you and loves you.

These two sisters, Mary and Martha, needed a miracle. They didn't need a doctor—too late for that. They needed the impossible. They needed a supernatural miracle.

This brings me to the next point: Restoration takes place in the supernatural realm. The work of the Holy Spirit is supernatural. It cannot be manufactured. It cannot be maneuvered. It cannot be made up. It's either all real or it's not real at all. All of God's work, in both the Old Testament and New Testament, is supernatural.

- God restores people, cities, and nations.
- God restores relationships, friendships, and fellowships.
- God restores bodies, souls, and spirits.

Do not fear the supernatural work of God but, instead, embrace it. Embrace it every time you pray. Embrace it with expectation. Embrace it as you read the Scriptures. Do not expect restoration to come only in the natural but also in the supernatural through prayers of faith, through expectation of the promises of God, through the power of the Holy Spirit.

Now let's get back to Lazarus. As I mentioned before, his name means "God has helped." You see, God identified Lazarus at birth. He was set apart for a holy purpose—that God might be glorified. You, too, are set apart for holy use—that God might be glorified. Set in your mind as you are facing the challenges of life that God will use your trials and tribulations for your good and that He will be glorified in it. Does that erase your pain? No, but there will come the understanding that there truly is purpose in your pain.

I Am

Jesus identified Himself to Martha. "Jesus said to her, 'I am the resurrection and the life. Those who believe in me, even though they die, will live, and everyone who lives and believes in me will never die. Do you believe this?'" (John 11:25-26 NRSV).

- I am the Resurrection.
- I am the Life.
- I came to give you life, and life more abundantly.
- I am the answer to your problem.
- I am big enough to deal with your issues today, not only in the sweet by-and-by, but today.

Jesus is staking His reputation on you having an eternal life. Do you believe it?

God has also identified you. He calls those who believe as the chosen, the elect, daughters, heirs, a royal priesthood, His treasured possession. Your identity and character will soon line up. That is why you must know who and what God calls you. If you are standing on a shaky foundation, you will have a much more difficult time during times of great struggles. If God has called you from the kingdom of darkness into the kingdom of light, if He has saved you and given you eternal life, if He has breathed His breath into your body and taken up residency in the form of the Holy Spirit, then trust that He has your best interest at heart. I ask you, if God is omnipresent, omniscient, omnipotent, He can deal with your life struggles. Rest knowing this truth. I do not say that lightly. I have had many dark days. I have faced tremendous life challenges and heartaches. I have walked on the path of sickness leading to potential death. I UNDERSTAND.

NUGGETS OF WISDOM: Behold, I lay in Zion for a foundation a stone, a tried stone, a precious cornerstone of a sure foundation. He who believes shall not act hastily. (Isaiah 28:16 WEB)

Restorative Power

To experience the fullness of God's restorative power, you must embrace the reality of the supernatural. "Martha then said to Jesus, 'Lord, if You had been here, my brother would not have died" (John 11:21). This is a measure of faith. "Even now," she said, "I know that whatever You ask of God, God will give you" (v. 22). Even greater faith. "Jesus said to her, 'Your brother will rise again'" (v. 23).

This was a call for the greatest of supernatural faith: above all reason, above all logic, above all of your reality, God is calling for supernatural faith. To experience the fullness of God's restorative power, you must embrace the reality of the supernatural. You must believe that God gives life and trust that God's power supersedes our reality. Reality is reality, but God's power supersedes our reality.

NUGGETS OF WISDOM: I will lift up my eyes to the mountains. Where will my help come from? My help comes from the Lord, Who made heaven and earth. (Psalm 121:1-2 NLV)

God helps us today—accept it, believe it, and receive it.

Are you more like Mary or Martha? Are you resting at His feet, or are you stopping short of your miracle because of unbelief? Perhaps you doubt His omnipotence, doubt His omnipresence, doubt His omniscience, or doubt His compassion to help you on this journey. God and His power are much greater than our reality. The Bible reads, "Jesus wept. So the Jews were saying, 'See how He loved him!' But some of them said, 'Could not this man, who opened the eyes of the blind man, have kept this man also from dying?'" (John 11:35-37).

You are not alone. You see, the Jews also questioned Jesus' power, nature, and motives. They were disappointed in Jesus. They were disappointed that He delayed coming to them. They were disappointed that their beloved brother had already passed. They were disappointed that Jesus did not make it on time. They were disappointed that Jesus was not going to pull this one off.

Are you filled with questions? Are you hurting because things aren't working out the way you had expected? Has life thrown you a curveball? Perhaps you've been disappointed. "God, where were You when . . .?" Just know this:

- God is on time.
- God will never leave or forsake you.
- God sees your pain.
- God knows your hurts.
- God understands your disappointments.
- God is working behind the scenes on your behalf.

Believe and receive His promises.

Jesus said to Martha, "Your brother will rise again" (John 11:23). "When He had said these things, He cried out with a loud voice, 'Lazarus, come forth'" (v. 43).

You may feel that things are hopeless, but if you will build your life on the assurance of Scripture, you will begin to see God at work in the midst of your darkness. You will see the little treasures He will send your way. You will feel His love in a new and deeper way. Watch God work. Look for those sweet signs of His never-ending compassion, His abounding mercy, and His freely given grace.

NUGGETS OF WISDOM: "I knew that You always hear Me; but because of the people standing around I said it, so that they may believe that You sent Me." When He had said these things, He cried out with a loud voice, "Lazarus, come forth." The man who had died came forth, bound hand and foot with wrappings, and his face was wrapped around with a cloth. Jesus said to them, "Unbind him, and let him go." (John 11:42-44)

Build Your Foundation

Start here, on a sure foundation. God accomplishes our restoration, salvation, justification, sanctification, and renewal through the power of the Holy Spirit because of the sacrificial blood of His Son, Jesus Christ. "The Lord is my rock and my fortress and my deliverer, My God, my rock, in whom I take refuge; My shield and the horn of my salvation, my stronghold" (Psalm 18:2).

Say this.

Believe this.

Stand on this.

Our ability to face trials, tribulations, suffering, sickness, or disease all rest in the power of God working through us, giving us all we need to get through it. This is a firm foundation that will stand when the storms of life come our way.

We decided not to invest in that house we had visited in Virginia. We were sure that the cost of repair would be far too substantial. As beautiful as it was on the outside, the inside was destroyed. Your life is the same. The losses are too great when built on a faulty foundation. It's a price you cannot afford to pay.

TREASURE CHEST

Spiritual laws do not change. God's Word is true. This is a sure foundation. You can build your life on it.

- Build your life on a firm foundation found in God's Word.

- We are spiritual beings that will go on into eternity.

- God is still working miracles today.

- Do not fear the supernatural—instead embrace it.

- Believe that Jesus brings dead things back to life.

- God is working even in the midst of your pain.

- God's timing is different than our timing, and His timing is perfect.

The Comforter has come,
the Comforter has come!
The Holy Ghost from Heav'n,
the Father's promise giv'n;
O spread the tidings 'round
wherever man is found—
The Comforter has come!

—Frank Bottome, "The Comforter Has Come"

CHAPTER 3

MY COMFORTER

Bailey, a dear friend and ministry partner, called me for prayer. She had been transported to a state far from my home to live with several family members in the final months of her battle with cancer. Her days were coming to an end, and she was dying. She was standing at heaven's gates. I remember praying with tears streaming down my face, asking the Lord to be her comfort. After the prayer she said to me, "I feel such tremendous peace." It was not long afterward that she went home to be with Jesus.

I can confidently tell you that had it not been for the precious Holy Spirit giving her heart comfort and peace, she would have had a much more difficult time facing those final days and hours ahead. She was a fully committed Christian and firmly understood that Jesus is the only way to the Father. Bailey had made things right with the people in her life with whom she had been at odds, and she was ready to be with Jesus. I can tell you, it's not always that way. I have personally watched individuals on their deathbeds who were not at peace. What is it that allows individuals to be able to face life's challenges, and even death, with such tremendous peace and comfort? In a word, it's Jesus' precious Spirit.

The Only Way

Jesus is the way, the truth, and the life. He is the source of resurrection power. He is the source of love, peace, and joy. He has dominion over the natural realm as He walked on water, healed the sick, opened blind eyes, and made the lame walk again. When Jesus went to be with God, He said He would send us our Helper, our Teacher, our Comforter—the Holy Spirit.

The Holy Spirit is part of the triune Godhead: Father, Son, and Holy Spirit. When you receive Christ as Savior, you then receive His Spirit into your heart and life. The Spirit dwells in you and longs to lead, guide, teach, and help you. You then must decide to yield to His leading. That becomes a little more challenging. We are used to being in charge of all that we think, all that we do, and all that we plan to do. When we truly yield to the influence of the Holy Spirit, we put our own desires, wants, and wishes in second place and allow the Spirit to lead. I know . . . OUCH!

One day, many years ago, I went to the refrigerator to get a glass of milk. I heard something in me say *no*, so I didn't get the milk. A little later I was going for crackers before lunch and again I heard *no*, so I didn't have the crackers either. Shortly thereafter, I reached for a cup for coffee. You guessed it. I heard the third *no* in a row, in my spirit. *Lord, what is going on?* I thought. Then I heard that still, small voice in my heart say, *I am teaching you how to hear my voice.* Oh, okay, I get it. What a revelation. It was through that still, small voice inside of me that God was teaching me to hear His voice. Just as a parent protects a child, the Holy Spirit was training me to listen and obey, no matter how small or insignificant the directive might have been. You see, it is often in the small things when we truly decide to follow or not. Then, when the bigger issues confront our lives, we are ready to handle them because we have been trained to obey. Obedience brings blessings, protection, and guidance when we learn to listen to the leadership of the Holy Spirit.

No matter how close our relationship with God is or how many times we go to church or even how often we pray for ourselves and our families, we all face challenges in our faith. We are challenged to the core of our being. We are shaken until we feel like we just cannot stand. Things happen to us that make us cry out, "Why, God? Why me?" and leave us wondering why bad things happen to good people.

SHAREWORTHY

When bad things happen to good people,
only the knowledge of a sovereign God will
quiet the anxious heart.

—Robin Bertram

Why, God

Have you ever wondered why some people, especially the righteous, have to endure hardships, trials, sickness, or disease? I've wondered. Of all the evil people in the world, why do God's people suffer? I have been asked this question over and over again and found the answer in the third chapter of Genesis.

Sin and rebellion brought troubles, sickness, disease, and death into this world. God's original plan was for man to walk in constant communion with Him—in peace, in health, and in wholeness. Sin introduced sickness and death, and man became cursed with the plague of death because of his rebellious acts against God. Sin also brought chaos and destruction into the world, and all are affected by it: the righteous and the unrighteous, the just and the unjust.

We tend to think that we are punished by God when we face challenges. We are not. Resist that temptation. Jesus said He came to give life—an abundant life. He did not say He came to bring sickness upon us or to bring destruction into our lives. Again, I repeat, you are not being punished. That being said, the unrighteous act of sin came through one man, Adam. The answer for our hardships came through another man, Jesus Christ.

We have hope, as believers and followers of Jesus Christ, in the midst of our questioning. God reconciled Himself to mankind through the life, death, burial, and resurrection of His Son Jesus Christ, thus restoring our personal relationship with God, which was broken through sin and rebellion during the fall of man. God puts His Spirit in us, and He is called to empower, to commission, to comfort, to guide, to lead, to instruct, to bring conviction, to sanctify us, and to impart spiritual truths. He also gives us His Spirit to strengthen our inner being during times of trial.

NUGGETS OF WISDOM: Oh Lord my God, I cried to You for help and You healed me. (Psalm 30:2 NLV)

The Sick Are Healed

Many years ago, I was asked to be one of the leaders for a weekend retreat for teens and young adults in southern Georgia. Lucas, a young man who joined us on our campus, had suddenly become very ill with a very high temperature. He had been sick throughout the night but thought things would change. However, they did not. We tried to reach his family, but there was no response to the numerous calls, and we were a good distance from a doctor or a hospital. One of the leaders felt led to pray for Lucas, so our team immediately gathered around him and began to pray for his healing. Within a few minutes, the fever left him. The next night this teen stood up in front of a large group of peers and visitors to share his experience. While he had grown up in the church, with his dad as pastor, he had never personally experienced the power of God so clearly until that very moment when he was healed. He gave God all the glory, and many youth gave their life to the Lord that very night. He knew the Lord in a new way, a deeper and more profound way.

NUGGETS OF WISDOM: And I will pray the Father, and he shall give you another Comforter, that he may abide with you for ever. (John 14:16 KJV)

Comfort in Knowing

The Holy Spirit is our Comforter, and there is great comfort that comes through knowing Him. How well do you know Him? Do you have intimacy with Him? As believers, we have hope through His Spirit. Hope is not wishful thinking; it is a decision based on a conviction or a fact based on truth found in Scripture. For the non-believer, there is no hope. However, as a believer, you know what will take place in your future. It is a settled thing and an unquestionable fact that you, once you accept Jesus as Lord, will have a glorified body one day and life eternal. You will not perish but live on into eternity. You might be asking yourself, "What does all this have to do with what I am going through right now?" It is vital in that, when storms, trials, or difficulties come your way, you know that you will hear His voice and be comforted.

> NUGGETS OF WISDOM: "My sheep hear My voice, and I know them, and they follow Me; and I give eternal life to them, and they will never perish; and no one will snatch them out of My hand."
>
> (John 10:27-28)

What challenges has the devil thrown your way? What hardships are you struggling with that seem insurmountable? What tragedies have you had to face? Do you feel as though God has abandoned you? There is only one way to get through the darkness, and that is by the power of the Holy Spirit who is working in those who have accepted Jesus Christ of Nazareth as Lord. Yield to Him now:

> Dear Heavenly Father,
>
> Thank You, Lord, for Your leadership in my life. I need Your help today. Help me to lean on Your Holy Spirit. Help me to rely on Your Spirit. Help me to know that what I am going through right now is not punishment

from You. I choose today to yield to Your Spirit and obey. I choose today to give You my cares, my burdens, and my pain. May You cover me in Your love, Your grace, and Your mercy. Empower me this day to see the treasures that You are sending my way, even in the midst of this darkness. May I receive them with peace, comfort, and joy. In Jesus' name I pray, amen.

Comfort in Hearing

My daughter, Taylor, is a treasure to me. She was a wonderful baby and an easy child to raise because she had a drive in her from the very beginning to always work hard and do things the right way. I love that about her. She is fun loving and full of energy. When she was a little girl, she went through a period complaining that her stomach ached. She was not a complainer, so we always took notice if she wasn't feeling well. After dealing with this for a while, I called her pediatrician, who recommended that we bring her in for testing. We did, but they could not find anything. Later, we were sent to the hospital for further testing, but again, nothing transpired. We prayed and asked God to show us what was going on with Taylor. One night, in the middle of the night, my husband sat up in bed and said, "It's lactose intolerance." Before our next visit to the hospital, we specifically asked our doctor to test for it, and sure enough, that's exactly what it was. We are confident that the Lord shed light on the situation. We prayed. He answered. God is good. He is willing to help us. He wants us to hear His voice.

SHAREWORTHY

God leads us to pray for a reason. Wisdom
tells us we need to do it.

—*Robin Bertram*

Comfort in His Spirit

God is supreme, and His Spirit rules and reigns above all, and in this we find comfort and peace. Who is the Holy Spirit? When Jesus went to heaven, He said He would leave us another, a Comforter. He fulfills the work of God in us. He strengthens us and empowers us. He renews and restores us. He seals us, meaning He marks us as belonging to God. Therefore, we are under His protection. The Holy Spirit has divine attributes ascribed to Him, such as supreme knowledge, sovereignty, and eternal existence. He, too, is all-knowing, ever-present, and all-powerful. The Holy Spirit is sometimes referred to as the Spirit of Truth, the Spirit of Christ, or the Spirit of God. He has an intellect. Attributed to Him are such divine works as creation and the process of being born again, or the New Birth. He is the revealer of divine truth. He convicts individuals of sin and prompts their hearts to change. He is the source of all life. That said, it is during times of severe distress when we need more than someone's kind word. We need the supernatural power of the Holy Spirit flowing through us to survive day by day. We need His grace flowing through us. We need His love to surround us. We need His peace to settle our frightened hearts. We need His precious Spirit to comfort us.

NUGGETS OF WISDOM: "As for Me, this is My covenant with them," says the Lord: "My Spirit which is upon you, and My words which I have put in your mouth shall not depart from your mouth, nor from the mouth of your offspring, nor from the mouth of your offspring's offspring," says the LORD, "from now and forever." (Isaiah 59:21)

Comfort in His Promises

When I was battling illness for a year and a half, I stood on God's promises: they were all I had. I had been so sick that, when I was only five minutes from my home, I couldn't find my way back. Making my bed was too great a challenge. Brushing my hair took more energy than I had. Day after day I felt myself getting weaker. I knew that this battle was far greater than what I could handle, so I went first to the church to be anointed with oil. I asked the leadership team to pray the prayer of faith over me for healing. I grabbed every promise written in the Word of God. I wrote those Scriptures down, and I declared them over and over. I reminded God that I was in covenant with Him and that He was a covenant-keeping God; He does not lie. He does not break His own Word, rather He watches over His Word to perform it.

Robin, are you going to believe what you've taught for the last thirty years, or are you going to give up and give in to this battle? I finally had to ask myself. *Do you believe?* This kept running through my head like a broken record. I knew it was God trying to get me to see that, yes, I did believe and I was ready to fight. *Thank You, Lord, for Your persistence.* His sweet Spirit kept prompting me to look into my own heart and determine what was actually there.

NUGGETS OF WISDOM: Then the LORD said to me, "You have seen well, for I am watching over My word to perform it." (Jeremiah 1:12)

The Snow Globe

I had received a call from a young woman who was struggling. Olivia was a Christian and attended church for several years, however, she felt very distant from God. She was struggling with her faith because she thought that if God really loved her, her life would have been going in a better direction. Olivia and her husband were having issues, and she was ready to just give up because she felt she was in total darkness.

My prayer partner and I gathered with Olivia and prayed over her. I remember looking into her sad eyes and all I could see was a little girl hovering in a dark corner of the room. I saw her little dress and shoes. I shared the vision, a gift from the Holy Spirit, with her, and sure enough, she had been an abused child. The darkness Olivia experienced was a direct result of the abuse she had encountered as a child, and that abuse was never adequately addressed. Although she knew God, she had been blaming Him for most of her life. It wasn't until she understood that God gives man free will and that the abuse was not God's will for her, that she could stop blaming Him and start receiving His love.

Olivia prayed a simple prayer of forgiveness, released her father from all the hurt and pain, and was totally healed of years of anger, depression, and despair. She could now believe the truth of Scripture and receive God as a perfect, loving Father. Those walls that kept God out were torn down, and His love came rushing in. Olivia was no longer in darkness but could see the light of God's love forever changed.

As we got up to leave, she glanced over and saw a little glass snow globe that her father had given her as a child. She was astounded and could not fathom who had put it there. Perhaps it was just a little treasure or sign that she was on the right path that day when she decided to give God her pain and sorrow and let Him take His rightful place as the perfect loving Father.

> NUGGETS OF WISDOM: In the same way the Spirit also helps our weakness; for we do not know how to pray as we should, but the Spirit Himself intercedes for us with groanings too deep for words. (Romans 8:26)

Today I challenge you to look at what God is doing in the midst of your own personal darkness. Ask yourself, *What has been a blessing to me today? What little joy have I experienced? What good has happened around me?* Then thank God for that good. Thank Him that He is with you. Thank Him that His Spirit dwells within you. When facing many of my own personal struggles, my comfort is found in knowing the voice of God, which takes a little practice. My comfort is found as I read and meditate on the truth of God's Word. My comfort is found as I choose to believe for the impossible when I am told it is useless. God's Spirit is my Comforter.

> NUGGETS OF WISDOM: When you pass through the waters, I will be with you. When you pass

through the rivers, they will not flow over you. When you walk through the fire, you will not be burned. The fire will not destroy you.

(Isaiah 43:2 NLV)

Signs of Hope

I used to work with a woman who had been in darkness. Sheila had been through a terrible divorce, lost her home, and had no place to live. She was at her wits' end. One day, as she was driving around in her car, she cried out to God in her distress. "God, please. I need Your help." Just then she looked up and happened to see a billboard that read, "Hope has a new address and it's yours." Sheila immediately declared, "That is just what I need." The sign also highlighted three words in the form of a hashtag: #HOPENOTWASTED. Those three words became her heart and her ministry call. Those statements became who she was and what she believed. Her life, her pain, her disappointment, and all the struggles were not in vain. God gave her, that day, a literal sign to bring her from the pit of despair into the place of abundance in Him, and she accepted it as a gift from God, a treasure that radically changed her vision and her life.

SHAREWORTHY

God sends us signs that He is with us, and He gives us His Word so we won't miss them.

—*Robin Bertram*

You or a dear family member might be going through a battle with cancer or some other illness. Perhaps you are going through a divorce, and your home and life have been ripped apart. Perhaps you have been physically or emotionally abused in your past. Maybe you need an answer about a problem you are facing. Whatever you are going through right now, what I can tell you for sure is that you need the power of the Holy Spirit to get you through. You need to hear His precious voice leading and guiding you. You need to know where you are going and how you are going to get there. Please, please, please, hear me. If you've never heard His voice or had an experience with the leading of the Holy Spirit, you can. You can hear His voice in your heart saying, "This is the way, now walk in it."

NUGGETS OF WISDOM: Blessed be the God and Father of our Lord Jesus Christ, the Father of mercies and God of all comfort, who comforts us in all our affliction so that we will be able to comfort those who are in any affliction with the comfort with which we ourselves are comforted by God. For just as the sufferings of Christ are ours in abundance, so also our comfort is abundant through Christ.
(2 Corinthians 1:3-5)

Time and time again, God has saved me from near misses, from potential dangers, from sicknesses, and even death. Bailey received comfort and peace in the time of her home going. Lucas got his physical healing, and the fever left his body. My daughter was diagnosed through divine revelation of the Holy Spirit. Olivia found comfort in seeing the snow globe, a childhood gift from her father. Sheila gained encouragement and guidance to move into her future, even after a life-shattering divorce, with confidence that God would be with her. Each of us moved forward and did so through the power of the Holy Spirit and His voice leading and guiding us along the way.

Do not miss what God is doing in the midst of your own personal darkness. Sometimes it is the smallest thing that gives the greatest hope. My heart is to bring you encouragement in the midst of your darkness and the assurance that God is right there with you, desiring to lead you through your time of difficulty. The Holy Spirit dwells in you, and this is the same Spirit that raised Christ Jesus from the grave. It is the same Holy Spirit that was there when God spoke the world into existence. It is the same Holy Spirit that seals us for the day of redemption. Do you know Him? If not, today is your day.

NUGGETS OF WISDOM: Now may the God of hope fill you with all joy and peace in believing, so that you will abound in hope by the power of the Holy Spirit. (Romans 15:13)

TREASURE CHEST

- Find comfort in knowing Jesus.

- Find comfort in the Holy Spirit, and know He is with and in you.

- Find comfort in His promises; they are true and everlasting.

- Find comfort as you learn to discern His voice; ask Him to help you.

- Find comfort in following the lead of the Holy Spirit, and decide to follow.

- Find comfort in Scriptures to bring hope in the midst of your own personal darkness by standing on them and declaring them over your situation.

- Find comfort in the little signs God sends all along the way.

PART TWO

LOOKING OUTWARD

Souls in danger, look above,
Jesus completely saves,
He will lift you by His love,
out of the angry waves;
He's the Master of the sea,
billows His will obey,
He your Savior wants to be,
be saved today.
Love lifted me!
Love lifted me!
When nothing else could help,
Love lifted me!

—James Rowe, "Love Lifted Me"

CHAPTER 4

Love Lifted Me

As I stood in my church during praise and worship, I turned and looked behind me and saw a group of small children, all from one family, singing as loudly as they could. I thought to myself, *That must be what love sounds like.* My son came into my house one day, and I had his favorite pot of soup on the stove. He turned and looked at me with the sweetest smile of contentment, and I thought to myself, *That must be what love smells like.* My little granddaughter was visiting and my husband, Ken, picked her up. She grabbed his face with her tiny little hands, and I thought to myself, *That must be what love feels like.*

SHAREWORTHY

Love is a force more powerful than death,
pure as gold, desired more than precious
jewels. It makes our trials bearable.

—*Robin Bertram*

You might recall the childhood song "Jesus Loves Me." You may have sung it in Sunday school, but do you believe it? I have ministered to people from all walks of life, and when you get real personal with someone, he or she will often share his or her deepest, most concealed thoughts. When trials and tribulations come, it is not uncommon to get mad at God, feel like He really does not love you, or even deny that He exists. Crisis may cause you to ask questions:

- "Where are You, God? Why I am going through all this? Why are You allowing this to happen to me?"
- "I serve You, yet why am I struggling?"
- "Why is my family falling apart?"
- "Why am I facing this disease?"
- "Why is my child dying?"

Are you or a loved one struggling with any of these questions?

SHAREWORTHY

In the midst of utter darkness, I cried out to God and shined His light into the deepest part of my soul. I could see again.

—*Robin Bertram*

In my own personal darkness, there were times when I cried out to God and asked these very questions, and I learned that it is at times like these that we have to stand on the truth of Scripture. We can't go by our feelings. Our feelings will lie to us. Our feelings will say, "I told you He didn't love you." We have to accept what has been written, trust in it, and guide our thoughts accordingly, not by how we feel, but on what is written. What if you do not believe what is written? Bow your head and ask God to make Himself real to you. Here and now, He will.

> NUGGETS OF WISDOM: If I say, "For sure the darkness will cover me and the light around me will be night," even the darkness is not too dark to You. And the night is as bright as the day. Darkness and light are the same to You.
>
> (Psalm 139:11-12 NLV)

The long and short of it is that we do live in a fallen world. We do live in physical bodies that are affected by environment, genetics, certain susceptibilities, and so on. Sin introduced sickness and disease. God is our loving Father who will either heal us or help us through it. There are some things we can never know while we are here in this body, and we won't know the "why" until we get to heaven. What we do know is that God is sovereign. He loves us because He is our Creator and Father. Peace comes when we truly know how much He loves us.

God Loves You

Do you believe that God loves you?

We cannot know the fullness of God's love until we first know God. While we were lost, living a life that was displeasing to God,

He still loved us and wanted the best for us. How do I know that for sure? Because the Bible tells me that Jesus died for me while I was still a sinner separated from God. God gave His Son as a payment for our sins: yours and mine. Can you imagine that kind of love? It is difficult for us to understand, but all sin has a cost, and God was willing to sacrifice Jesus on a cross, shedding His precious blood to pay the penalty for our sins once and for all. It is through that decision that we can come to God and experience His love.

> NUGGETS OF WISDOM: And he said to him, "You shall love the Lord your God with all your heart and with all your soul and with all your mind. This is the great and first commandment. And a second is like it: You shall love your neighbor as yourself."
> (Matthew 22:37-39 ESV)

Love God. Love your neighbor. Love yourself. To love God is to keep His commandments. To love God with a genuine love is to abhor evil and hold fast to what is good. To know God is to receive His love. When you or a loved one are going through a difficult time or have been diagnosed with a debilitating, long-term, or potentially fatal disease, when you are in the midst of utter darkness, the most important thing needed is an overwhelming sense of love and compassion from God, from family, and from friends.

In support of those who are struggling, it's imperative to make an effort to spend time with them. Hold their hand, rub their back, or read a book to them. It's minimizing stress and giving encouragement. It's bringing a small gift or sending a card. It's making a telephone call regularly when you cannot be there personally. Love will help you or your loved one fight through the battle. It is more than merely saying the words; it is putting emotions into action.

SHAREWORTHY

Do ordinary things with extraordinary love.
—*Mother Teresa*

Lead in Love

Now is the time for everyone in the family to come together. Someone needs to lead the way, especially when there is division. Take that step. Make those calls. Tell family members to let bygones be bygones. There is no time for selfishness, pride, or a need to be proven as being *right* from old disputes. Proof is in your actions not your words. Surround your loved one with great love. Love can keep you moving forward and not giving up.

I once sat by the hospital bed of a man who had been very ill for a number of years. He was determined to fight because he had a wife and four beautiful children whom he wanted to take care of. He suffered greatly but could not let go of life. The love he had for his family was stronger than the disease that racked his body. His precious wife looked into his eyes and told him she and the children would be fine and that he could go be with Jesus. He gently nodded, took his last breath, and entered the gates of heaven. Love expressed at those moments creates treasures that will impact everyone involved.

These lingering moments of joy will resound long after a loved one is gone. We surrounded his hospital bed and sang beautiful old hymns of praise. A servant had gone home.

Love God, Love People

"'You shall love your neighbor as yourself.' There is no other commandment greater than these" (Mark 12:31). That means to purposefully choose to interact with everyone you encounter with the love of God. Have the heart of Christ, and love your neighbor as yourself. You may ask, "How do I do that? You don't know my neighbor." We cannot love the unlovely outside of God's grace and mercy flowing through us. We can only love the unlovely because God gives us the ability to do so through the power of the Holy Spirit working in the life of every believer.

SHAREWORTHY

Love is a reflection of God in us.

—*Robin Bertram*

I have a great friend who thrives on taking up the challenge to be Christlike. When she knows someone doesn't particularly care for her, she makes every effort to extend love to him or her. She'll hug them when she sees them. She'll say, "I love you," to them, all the while knowing that they may not really care for her. She simply takes a negative and turns it into a positive. Not everyone becomes her friend as a result, but she knows in her heart that, above all, she is pleasing God. What a great way to live. Augustine, an early Christian theologian and philosopher once said, "Inasmuch as love grows in you, in so much beauty grows; for love is itself the beauty of the soul."[1] Love is the beauty of the soul. It is also a reflection of God because God is love.

> NUGGETS OF WISDOM: Loving-kindness and truth have met together. Peace and what is right and good have kissed each other.
>
> (Psalm 85:10 NLV)

Righteousness and Peace Kiss

Jesus wants us to be influential for His kingdom and taught the power of love through His actions. Remember the woman caught in adultery (see John 8:1-11)? After being caught in the very act, an angry mob surrounded her with stones in their hands, ready to kill her. She laid in the dirt with tears of terror streaming down her face when Jesus bent down to write something in the sand. The Pharisees were testing Jesus as He wrote on the ground. They must have been thinking, *This is our right. This is our law. This is our duty.* But Jesus said to them, "He who is without sin among you, let him be the first to throw a stone at her" (John 8:7). Then Jesus said, "'Woman, where are they? Did no one condemn you?' She said, 'No one, Lord.' And Jesus said, 'I do not condemn you, either. Go. From now on sin no more.'" (vv. 10-11).

It was a time and place where the Old Testament collided with the New Testament: stoning versus freedom, law versus grace, mercy versus judgment. This woman must have felt a great sense of relief, like a near miss or like being pulled from a burning building. Perhaps it felt like being on the tracks in front of an oncoming train with no way to get off, and then the Savior walked onto the scene. He displayed the greatest mercy of God in His greatest glory toward all mankind as he demonstrated love, forgiveness, and compassion. This woman was saved from judgment, which was stoning, the law of the land. The hand of Jesus healed her spiritually as He said, "Now go and sin no more, so something worse won't happen to you." Woman, you are freed. No judgment here. You have been acquitted. Jesus said, "Go . . . sin no more." Now that you see Me and understand My character and My nature, "Go . . . sin no more." What a tremendous act of love this woman experienced. If Jesus can love us even in our mess, then we should learn to love ourselves. Now is the time to deepen your love walk, and here are four steps that will help you on your journey.

SHAREWORTHY

God loves each of us as if there were only
one of us.
—*St. Augustine (attributed)*

Love Yourself

Step One

Understand that God's love is unconditional, pure, and without limits. Accept His love. True and pure love is about sacrificing for others. God loved us so much that He gave us His Son as payment for our sins. He loves us so much that He will never leave us nor forsake us. He loves us so much that He made us alive together with Christ, and when we have been born again, we are promised life eternal. How can we not love a God who loves us so much?

Step Two

Forgive yourself for poor decisions. Forgive yourself for wrong actions. Forgive yourself for your wrong relationships. Now your slate is wiped clean, and you can no longer go back and hold yourself captive to all of the past mistakes that you've made. How can you learn to love yourself? You can start by understanding how God truly sees you. If God Almighty calls you His treasure, the apple of His eye, and His beloved, then how can you exalt your opinion over His decision? Many people go through life feeling totally inadequate and insufficient, wishing that they were different. However, God said He knitted you together when you were in your mother's womb. He said you were fearfully and wonderfully made. He said you are His treasured possession. There is no time like the present to truly take on that identity.

Step Three

Do not look at your life and judge it as a failure. This is a trick of the devil, meant to deceive you. Your steps have been determined. Remember that the past is gone. It's never too late to be forgiven of the sins of your past. Simply confess them to God. You are then forgiven and accepted into the family.

Step Four

Realize there is a reason for your life and your pain. God has a plan for it all. There is nothing wasted. "For surely I know the plans I have for you, says the LORD, plans for your welfare and not for harm, to give you a future with hope" (Jeremiah 29:11 NRSV).

SHAREWORTHY

What does love look like? It has the hands to help others. It has the feet to hasten to the poor and needy. It has eyes to see misery and want. It has the ears to hear the sighs and sorrows of men. That is what love looks like.
—*St. Augustine*

Being Present Is a Present

When you have a loved one who is struggling with real-life issues, loss, sickness, or a serious long-term disease, honor their requests. Being present is a real gift. Be loving. Encourage restoration. Encourage communication. When my mother-in-law went home to be with Jesus, my son, Logan, and daughter, Taylor, went to her bedside to spend the last week with her in the hospital. One day she woke up and saw her bed surrounded by her family. She smiled and said, "It looks like we are having a party!" Those moments were a treasure to Marie, and I know they were for Logan and Taylor. It meant the world to Marie to have her family present. If you are struggling right now from loss and hope has been stolen from you, consider connecting with loved ones. Communicate your needs to them; speak up and be honest with them.

Connect

Make relationships right. When you love God and love your neighbors as yourself, you have fulfilled the greatest of all commandments. Loving yourself becomes an important part of the equation. You see, it's very difficult to love others when you cannot love yourself. Choose to make relationships right by starting with your relationship with God and then with others. Connect with estranged loved ones or old friends from the past. Be that person who reaches out first. Connect and communicate.

Communicate

When someone is truly suffering, avoid these platitudes:

- God willed it.
- Every cloud has a silver lining.
- God needs one more flower in his garden.
- You'll be up and around in no time.
- You are going to be just one more bright star in the sky.

These platitudes are trite and offer no real sense of hope. While honesty is vitally important during these difficult times, avoid being brutally open in front of your loved one. Constantly reminding those who are ill of the finality of their situation can be very disturbing.

False Hope

Avoid giving false hope. It is much more productive to encourage your loved one to treasure every moment, regardless of circumstances. False hope may discourage the individual from taking necessary action or from facing the inevitable. You can offer hope through praying according to what is desired. If healing is desired, pray for a miraculous healing. If comfort is desired, pray for comfort. If peace is desired, pray for peace. Real hope is truly found in the midst of heartfelt prayer.

Do Not Be Disingenuous

Avoid being fake. *Happy, happy, happy* is not the face your precious loved one wants to see day after day. Real tears of sorrow show love. Do not hold back when you feel like crying. It is important to share true emotions as never before. This can be a real treasure at heaven's gates as your loved one sees you honestly working through the pain you are experiencing. It is only by His grace that both of you can get through, and knowing that in advance will ease the pressure to try to figure it all out.

Right to Speak Up

It is critical to give those who are struggling, sick, or dying the right to speak, especially those who are terminally ill. Many times individuals will speak as if their loved one cannot hear. They will also frequently answer questions instead of allowing the individual who is ill to respond. Those who are sick or fighting terminal illness must have a voice. If they doubt the potential of receiving their healing, then they should be allowed to say so. If they are fearful, they must be allowed to say so. They may just simply need to let someone know for reassurance. Oftentimes I have heard loved ones say, "Now don't talk like that; you are going to be fine." The problem with such statements is that they inhibit true feelings from being expressed and deeper issues from coming to the surface. The importance of communication cannot be overstated. It is probably the most important element in the dying process. While some statements are hard for family members to hear, it is a must for those who are terminal. The family may not know how to respond, and that is okay. Sometimes silence is the only proper response.

Be Honest

Honesty is also important. Sharing your fears, disappointments, and concerns with one another is a healthy way to get through the process. The sharing of honest feelings allows for healing. It opens the door for forgiveness as well as for a more intimate relationship. The wife of a dying friend stated, "I have no regrets." She said, "I did everything I could do. I kept him comfortable. I took care of him and met his every need. I don't know how to describe it, but I am at peace."

I witnessed this man frequently tell his precious wife how much she had meant to him. He told her over and over again how much he appreciated the constant care she had given him. There was a sweet, sweet presence in the room as he looked over at his treasure. The love he verbalized through his words had become seed for her recovery. Those words became the very thing that brought about healing from the grief she had experienced in her loss; a treasure at heaven's gates. When dealing with someone who is facing an illness or who is terminal, remember these suggestions:

- Allow your loved one to say what they are thinking.
- It's okay to not know what to say.
- It is okay to just be quiet.
- Be open and honest with your feelings when appropriate.
- Do not be flippant.
- Do not force the conversation.
- Do not use clichés or platitudes or force a joke into the conversation.

When we are faced with major life challenges, we often look around and see our pool of close friends begin to narrow. People are afraid to come. Many do not know what to say, how to help, or what to do. Sometimes they think they are a bother, or they just don't want to wear anyone out. Loneliness sets in, but remember, Jesus is there, right in the midst of struggle, pain, and sorrow. You need to reach out for help when help is needed, and remember these truths listed below:

- Stand on truth when nothing makes sense (see Romans 8:38-39). For the believer, God was there, is there, and will be there.
- Nothing is wasted (see Romans 5:2-5). God will use even our suffering and pain for our own good and for His glory.

- There is peace in knowing that we are truly loved by God (see 1 John 4:9-11). He was willing to sacrifice for us that we would have eternal life.

Jesus was moved with compassion to heal (see Mark 1:41). Holding out for a supernatural healing is an instrument of hope, which will help you or your loved one flourish in difficult times. This certainly does not discount the use of medical doctors. God uses them, too.

SHAREWORTHY

Darkness cannot drive out darkness; only light can do that. Hate cannot drive out hate; only love can do that.

—*Martin Luther King Jr.*

Love, love, love—as long as you have breath, love. We all show love in different ways; but it's not *how* we show love, it's that we *do* show love. Life can throw you a curveball, and sickness, long-term, or terminal illness is certainly an unexpected invader of your life. It tries to take over everything you are, everything you were, and everything you want to be. It leaves you shaken to the core of your being. It steals hope from your heart if you let it. This is the time to dig deep. Decide in your heart what is most important. Think about who has loved you and who you have loved. Let that be your strength. Let it be your passion. Let it be your guide. Love can keep you going when nothing else can.

The good news in all this is that you do not have to stop living. Your illness does not have to take center stage. It does not have to rule your life. Yes, you may have major life changes that you might have to make, but you can proceed with the joy of knowing who holds your future. God has the final say. I am living proof of that.

SHAREWORTHY

An ordinary friend will walk with you in the best of times. An extraordinary friend will walk with you in the worst of times.

—*Robin Bertram*

Show Love Through Treasured Memories

Encourage old friends to reminisce of days long past. Good times are important to remember. Such memories bring joy, laughter, and happiness and help to lift the burden and ease the pain, even if just for a short time. Take out the family pictures. Look at old slides or family movies. Invite old friends from the past to visit.

Show Love by Making Memories

Youth who are facing long-term or terminal illness are more interested in making memories. It is a wonderful time to plan a trip or plan to do something never experienced before. Making memories for the young and old should not stop but should continue as long as the individual is physically capable. For the youth, make a way to see the unseen if possible. Encourage them to do something they have never done before. This will allow for the anticipation of something new and exciting, which will help in giving relief from the mundane. It will also take the focus off of the situation for a time.

Show Love by Saving Memories

For the middle-aged, it is important that they have something of value to pass on to their children. Help them write some form of a memoir. They may want to include the values they hold dear or standards they want to set for their children. They may want to write down life lessons to share with the children or advice they would like to give. Encourage them to make videos of what is most important to them for the future of their children. Encourage them to make new memories, new friends, and new experiences.

For the elderly, encourage old friends from their past to come for a visit. Bring out old photographs or home movies, and enjoy watching them together. At the end of this book, you will find more suggestions listed in "Love in Action," which can be shared with friends and family to help through these difficult times.

My father was in the hospital the last week of his life. An old friend that he used to sing with walked in the door. Dad looked up and began to cry. Joy was written all over his face as the two old friends embraced. They reminisced about the days long past. They used to sing the old hymn "Love Lifted Me" when they were traveling together singing in a gospel quartet. Never underestimate the power of love and the importance of its effects.

What is love? Where do we find love? The Bible tells us that God is love and we find it in and through His Son, Jesus. That love is available no matter what stage of life we are in or what we may be going through. It is His love that will get us through the darkest of days. It is His love that will lead us home.

> NUGGETS OF WISDOM: Put me over your heart and on your arm, never to be taken off. For love is as strong as death. Jealousy is as hard as the grave. Its bright light is like the light of fire, the very fire of the Lord. Many waters cannot put out love. Rivers cannot cover it. If a man were to give all the riches of his house for love, it would all be hated. (Song of Solomon 8:6-7 NLV)

TREASURE CHEST

- Remember that God loves you no matter the circumstance.

- Remember that you need to love others and you need to receive their love.

- Remember that you also need to love yourself.

- Remember to connect, communicate, lead, and minister in love.

- Remember to give voice and allow your loved one to speak up.

- Remember to enjoy old friends, old memories, and old experiences.

- Remember to make new friends, new memories, and new experiences.

My hope is built on nothing less
Than Jesus' blood and righteousness;
I dare not trust the sweetest frame,
But wholly lean on Jesus' name.
On Christ, the solid Rock, I stand;
All other ground is sinking sand.

—Edward Mote, "My Hope Is Built
on Nothing Less"

CHAPTER 5

Hope Floats

Children have an uncanny way of believing by faith. You can tell a young child almost anything and they will believe you. I remember, as a young child, my siblings told me that I was adopted, and then my son told his sister, my daughter, the same thing and she believed him.

There is a tremendous beauty in the ability of a child to accept and hold on to truth when given the opportunity. I once worked with a young child who knew that when she closed her eyes here on earth, she would open her eyes in the presence of Jesus in heaven. Conversely, I distinctly remember sitting at the bedside of a pastor who was terrified at the process of death. What was the difference between these two individuals? In my mind and experience, the child didn't have the experience of doubt, while the adult had lots of practice. Wouldn't you love to live that way? Without doubt, I mean. We can live that way, but to do so we need to understand biblical hope.

Biblical Hope

Anne Graham Lotz once said, "If God can bring blessing from the broken body of Jesus and glory from something that's as obscene as the cross, He can bring blessing from my problems and my pain and my unanswered prayer. I just have to trust Him."[1] Biblical hope is an unshakable expectation that something good is going to happen . . . even something good will come out of something that is bad. Biblical hoping is believing that God works all things together for good for those who are called according to His purposes. It's the belief that there is a future with and in Jesus regardless of circumstances. Worldly hope today is more like wishful thinking. Can you see the difference?

SHAREWORTHY

Biblical hope is not merely acting as if it were positive thinking or a calculated wager, but a confident expectation in what is written.

—*Robin Bertram*

Where do you find hope when there is no hope to be found? How can you face daunting challenges when the doctor says, "There is nothing else we can do"? Do you turn to unconventional treatments? Do you go for the all-natural route: vitamins, supplements, or liquid diets? Do you seek out faith healers? Do you just give in and give up? After working with many sick and dying, as well as going through the possibility myself, I can tell you with all sincerity that only you can determine the path you will walk; not your spouse, not your children, not your pastor, and not even your doctor in many cases. You and you alone must decide.

People tend to heal quicker, stay longer, and accomplish important things that they want to accomplish before they leave this world when they stand in faith and have hope that at any point along the way, God can intervene and change things. Is that a pie-in-the-sky mentality? No, absolutely not. It is a healthy way to deal with the daily suffering and pain. The other option is to have no hope at all, which guarantees that the days will be long and difficult.

Martin Luther King Jr. said, "We must accept finite disappointment, but never lose infinite hope."[2] Yes, things happen, even bad things, but we can have hope even in the midst of tragedy.

SHAREWORTHY

My circumstances are very small in the eyes of
a very big God.

—*Robin Bertram*

Finding Hope

Hope is an essential and fundamental element of Christianity. Our hope is a reflection of the trust we have in God and our confidence in His Word. The biblical definition of hope in noun form is "expectation," and it indicates what is sure or certain.[3] In verb form, it is "expect with confidence."[4] It does not carry the same meaning that we tend to use today. In other words, it's not wishful thinking but again is a confident expectation of what is certain.

Where is your expectation level right now? Can you hope for the promises written in the Holy Bible? Can you stretch your thinking and expect good to come in the midst of darkness? Here are a few suggestions that have helped me when I was struggling: stay away from naysayers, find hope in association with hope-filled friends, put your hope solely in Jesus, grow in hope through hearing the Word of God, and trust that God is in it with you.

SHAREWORTHY

Circumstances are forever changing, but foundational truths never change; they become an anchor for our soul.

—*Robin Bertram*

Away with Naysayers

Have you ever had a friend or relative who calls you on the telephone just to complain about his or her life? It can be very draining. Or perhaps you've been around someone who always sees the glass half empty. There is never enough. Life is always bad. If you walk with naysayers, you will most likely become a naysayer. If you walk with people who always see the glass half empty, you, too, will see the glass half empty. If you associate with a positive, uplifting person, you will be more likely to be positive yourself. You become like those with whom you associate. This negative mind-set will strain even the most confident, fun-loving individual. Real-life associations matter. You may want to close the door on all those naysayers, those doubt-filled, weak-minded people who offer nothing but their sympathy.

> NUGGETS OF WISDOM: This hope we have as an anchor of the soul, a *hope* both sure and steadfast and one which enters within the veil.
>
> (Hebrews 6:19)

When I faced the potential of a terminal illness, I literally felt like I was dying. I chose to tell just a limited few. I chose to confide in just a small group of friends and family. Clearly, I remember the day that I shared with a family member a good report from my doctor. Her response astounded me. She literally became angry and accused me of not telling the truth about my report. This woman should have shouted for joy. She should have praised God for a good report. She should have been elated. Needless to say, she showed her true nature and from that day on was excluded from my inner circle. Although I chose to forgive her, I needed to be surrounded with faith-filled, kind, loving people. Naysayers will cost you more than you will want to pay. Simply walk away.

Finding Hope in Hope-Filled People

There were times throughout the life of Christ where He carefully selected those who would surround Him. There is an account in the Bible where Jesus was asked to go to the home of Jairus, one of the rulers of the synagogue, because Jairus's little girl was sick. Not knowing his daughter had already died, Jairus fell at the feet of Jesus and begged Him to come and just lay His hands on his daughter "so that she will get well and live" (Mark 5:23). Here, we see hope in action. There was an expectation in Jairus's heart that through the laying of hands, Jesus Christ could heal her. Even after she died, Jesus showed that he could raise this little girl up from death to life.

You will find this remarkable account in Mark 5:21-43. Jesus saw the pain in Jairus's face. He understood the severity of the situation and did not make light of it. Jesus cleared the room. He told all the mourners to get out and allowed only His chosen few—the parents and several of His disciples—to stay. Jesus had great compassion and said, "'Do not be afraid . . . only believe'" (v. 36). We, too, have to build our faith—not on something but on someone, and that *someone* is Jesus Christ. Someone once said, "Give a dying man a Bible. It's the only book he will ever need." Why? Because truth is the road map to peace, love, joy, healing, and life eternal.

> NUGGETS OF WISDOM: Trust in the Lord with all your heart, and do not trust in your own understanding. Agree with Him in all your ways, and He will make your paths straight.
>
> (Proverbs 3:5-6 NLV)

Hope in Jesus

Jesus took the girl by the hand, and in his native tongue he cried out, "'*Talitha kum!*'" which means "'Little girl, I say to you, get up!'"

(Mark 5:41). The Bible tells us that she immediately got up and began to walk. This young girl was completely restored from death to life, and yes, everyone there was completely astounded. *There is hope. There is hope. There is hope.*

Jesus sent His disciples out to heal the sick, to deliver people from the demonic influence, and to share the gospel. Clearly, healing was a major part of the work He expected out of His students and followers. Why should we follow His model? We should follow the model laid out in Scripture because Jesus brings hope and healing to a lost and dying world. We would do well to follow the example of Jairus also. It was his faith, his expectation of Jesus, that was the impetus for the miracle in the first place.

Hope Through Hearing

Perhaps you have a sick child. Your child will see your worry, your doubt, and your fears. Please understand, I am not suggesting that you fake it, but what I am suggesting is that you do your part. You, as a parent of a sick child, should do all you can to build your own faith and help them build theirs also.

Jairus, I am sure, heard of all the miraculous acts that Jesus performed. Jesus made His presence known everywhere He went because He was known for changing situations. Jesus was known for making the blind see, the deaf hear, the lame walk, and the dead be raised, both spiritually and physically. Jairus was basing his hope and his expectations on what he had already heard about Jesus and all that Jesus had done. Jairus believed because he had heard. Jesus changes situations. That said, do you, in your own heart, believe that Jesus changes situations?

I remember praying for a young girl who had been given a deadly diagnosis and was told that she only had several months to live. She was still somewhat able to get around on her own and loved to get outside as often as possible. She said it made her feel almost normal. She, her mother, and I would take short excursions, which, for the most part, would really lift her spirits. However, I noticed a trend that began in her mother, which was extremely hurtful to this young girl: Her mother would find it necessary to explain their situation everywhere we went. If a clerk at Macy's would listen, her mom would give her the complete rundown. It was same for the hairdresser, the grocery store checkout attendant, the postmaster, and on and on. One day we were at the beauty salon, and her mother began to share the whole story of her daughter's sickness, when out of the blue the child screamed out, "Mama, stop. I am not sick. Stop telling everyone that I am sick." Everyone just stopped in their tracks and stared at this child. She was right. She did not need to be reminded every day of her illness. She needed to feel normal.

There were several things going on here. One: the mother needed to vent her fear, anxiety, and pain. Two: her daughter wanted to just feel like a normal child. Three: the young girl did not want to be labeled as deathly ill over and over again. I share this story because when a child is struggling with an illness, parents would do well to learn to vent their fears and anxieties to professionals who can help them work through them: a pastor, a spiritual mentor, or even a good friend. Identifying your own feelings in a given situation is always a challenge. Mature Christian friends can help out in that area. They can be a sounding board or a very soft shoulder. To those who are struggling, others may not know what you need. You need to tell them what you need. Today, perhaps, you just need a hug, a cup of coffee, or a break from the heaviness of the current situation you find yourself in. Speak out your needs. Let your family and friends know.

Hope in Words

Now let's flip that situation around. Parents or loved ones speaking faith, praying faith, proclaiming faith offer their child or loved one real hope based on eternal, God-given principles. It is a proven fact that people will fight through loss, disease, divorce, and many other kinds of tragedy when there is a glimmer of hope.

There was once a dear friend who had a terminal illness, and I had the privilege of walking with him up to the final hours of his life. He used to say, "I hate this disease, and I am going to fight it." He had determined in his mind to make the disease an enemy instead of a friend. He would often talk to it as though it were an invader that must leave. This approach may not be right for everyone, but for him, I am confident it added years to his life. He decided that he would manage the rest of his life with proper diet and a natural holistic approach, which would involve vitamins and a litany of rituals in his daily routine. He emptied his cabinets of all chemicals. He bought organic foods. He bathed in natural products. He decided to refuse the prescribed medical treatment. His family thought he had lost his mind, but the doctors gave him no hope and told him that the treatment would not heal him. Hope will not disappoint because the love of God has been poured out into our hearts. My friend had hope. He would say, "If I am healed here or healed there, either way, I am healed." Powerful. What a beautiful attitude to hold firm. I asked him, "How long should I pray for healing?" His response, "Robin, as long as there is breath in my body." And that's what we did. Where can you find hope in the midst of such challenges? Draw near to God; there is great hope in His words.

> NUGGETS OF WISDOM: Heal me, O Yahweh, and I shall be healed; save me, and I shall be saved,: for you are my praise. (Jeremiah 17:14 WEB)

Hope in Partnership

God wants a partnership with you. He wants to grab you by the hand and lead you through. You are not alone. God promises throughout His Word that He will never leave or forsake you. You are not alone. You can draw near to Him by simply sitting in His presence with an open heart and a closed mouth. Why do I say that? Well, because if you do all the talking, how can you hear His directives? You may want to rise early in the morning, same time, same place, and meet with Him. Start out by welcoming Him. Ask Him to have His way and direct your life. Ask Him to speak to you and then, with hopeful expectation, listen and receive. You will find tremendous peace and hope in those moments of silence. The world may be swirling around your head. Your life might feel like it could crash in at any moment, but God and His sweet, sweet presence will offer more to you than anything else you could possibly do.

NUGGETS OF WISDOM: A man who does what is right and good may have many troubles. But the Lord takes him out of them all. (Psalm 34:19 NLV)

Hope in Tragedy

Turning tragedy into triumph is no small thing. Recently, I had the privilege of hearing the testimony of a woman who did just that. This precious lady had lost her sight as a young woman, found out her husband had been in an adulterous affair, and then experienced the loss of her eldest son in a stabbing incident. Yet this precious woman gave glory to God for her life. She had a very sweet spirit and traveled across the country encouraging other women in their faith. As I sat there listening to her, with tears rolling down my cheeks, I began to pray, "God forgive me for grumbling and complaining about my own life's issues." Her story touched me deeply and reminded me that there is always purpose in our pain. What did I take away from her story? I took away the fact that in our weaknesses, we are made strong through Christ Jesus. In our sorrows, He is our comfort. The Christian life is not meant to be without problems or without trials. God promises when we go through difficulties He will be with us. If we belong to Christ, then even our trials will bring Him praise, and it is in this that we are truly triumphant.

NUGGETS OF WISDOM: In this you greatly rejoice, even though now for a little while, if necessary, you have been distressed by various trials, so that the proof of your faith, being more precious than gold which is perishable, even though tested by fire, may be found to result in praise and glory and honor at the revelation of Jesus Christ.

(1 Peter 1:6-7)

Hope When All Is Lost

Look at the story found in Job 1:6–2:8. There is no greater picture of tragedy and the hope that emerges than that found in the Book of Job. What once used to be my least favorite book, I now understand and treasure the wisdom it offers. Job was acquainted with tragedy. We see the age-old debate emerging throughout the story. If God is so good, why do innocent people have to suffer?

Job was a very wealthy and influential sheikh. He had flocks and herds and an abundance of food, family, and fellowship. All who knew him held him in high esteem. Job was also a righteous man, a man who believed in and trusted God. However, his faith was shaken to the core after the loss of his family, his possessions, and his physical health. His wife, frustrated with all the chaos, challenged him to literally "curse God and die" (Job 2:9). Job's so-called friends chose to blame his tragic experiences on his own secret sinfulness. Thus, they argued, since Job is suffering so much, surely he must be a sinful man. However this, as we eventually find out, was simply not the case. Imagine for a moment what it must have felt like to be in Job's sandals. Battles, fire, and turbulent weather wiped out his vast fortune and killed his children. To add insult to injury, his body was covered in indescribably painful boils, and he himself was near death.

In the Book of Job, we find that he chose to believe in the Lord even when everyone around him thought differently. In his darkest hours, he acknowledged God's sovereignty. He could have taken his wife's advice to curse God, but he didn't. His response was, "You are talking like a foolish woman. Shall we accept good from God, and not trouble?" The Bible says that "In all this, Job did not sin in what he said" (Job 2:10 NIV). While Job certainly struggled with his own personal loss and his suffering throughout the book, he ultimately chose to look deep within and determined to find God in a deeper way. He wanted to understand. However, left in the dark as to the reason for his own suffering, Job decided his faith in God's goodness would stand. Job made a courageous choice to trust God in the midst of tragedy. This impoverished man could have railed against God, as his wife suggested, or he could have followed his friends' unwise advice and searched for some hidden, unconfessed sin, which deserved divine punishment. He didn't do that either because neither of those actions would have been fruitful. Instead, Job acknowledged God's right to do to him whatever God desired for the glory of His name (see Job 1:21). God chose Job to be tried and tested in the fire of refinement, and Job would find God in a more intimate way than he had ever known God before.

Why do the righteous suffer? The truth is it rains on the just and the unjust. Suffering builds and refines our faith. Suffering proves the genuineness of our faith. Suffering is a tool used as a witness of our faith.

NUGGETS OF WISDOM: And not only this, but we also exult in our tribulations, knowing that tribulation brings about perseverance; and perseverance, proven character; and proven character, hope. (Romans 5:3-4)

Hope in Confident Assurance

How do you know if you have enough faith to get through a situation like these we've discussed here? It is nearly impossible to know how strong your faith is until you are forced to depend on it. There are dimensions to our self-understanding and to our realization of what a relationship with God is all about that only emerge as we come face to face with our own doubts, questions, and introspection. It is in that place that we find out who God really is to us and who we really are to God.

God restored everything Job had lost. We find at the end that Job was not serving God for what God could give him, as he was first accused, but Job served God out of a true desire to please his God. What about you, friend? If your life is hit with sudden tragedy, how will you respond? Is your faith deep enough? Is your trust in God great enough to get you through tragedy, or are you simply going through the motions?

SHAREWORTHY

My faith isn't reliant on my own sufficiency;
it is reliant on the all-sufficient God who is
willing for all who are willing to believe.
—*Robin Bertram*

Here's your invitation. Choose today to trust God in all things. Accept His sovereign will for your life by understanding that God is truly in control. Perhaps you have already given up on God because of the tragedy you now face in your life. My friend, now is the day to turn that around. Learn to expect good things in your life even if you are in the midst of a storm. Determine to enjoy every day to the best of your ability. Determine to enjoy the small things in life: the sound of rain, the sunshine, or the smell of fresh coffee being brewed. You can have victory in knowing that God has you in the palm of His hand. Believe in God's faithfulness. Believe that God can turn your tragedy into triumph, no matter the outcome.

Several years ago, there was a movie written called *Hope Floats*. It was about a woman who was devastated by a divorce and her struggles to hope for love again. Hope is not ethereal. It is not wishful thinking. It is faith in action that stands firmly on Jesus Christ. It is built on a solid foundation, and it is sustained by love, truth, and the knowledge that, through Jesus Christ, hope is eternal and hope does not disappoint.

Lilly was in her late seventies when the man of her dreams, her faithful husband of fifty-five years, passed. He had given her a bouquet of roses every year on their anniversary with a note that said "Forever yours." After his death, the day of their anniversary came, and there was a knock at the door. A beautiful bouquet was delivered on her front porch. Lilly did not even take the time to read the note but rushed to the phone and called the local florist. She was quite angry, thinking the florist had made a terrible mistake. Calmly, the florist explained that her husband had prepaid for many years in advance to ensure that his dear, sweet wife would continue to receive the flowers on their special day. Lilly, with tears in her eyes, went outside and picked up the beautiful bouquet. It read "Eternally yours!"—a beautiful treasure found at the gates of heaven.

TREASURE CHEST

- Find hope in Jesus; He is the anchor of our soul.

- Find hope in words aptly spoken and words already written.

- Find hope as you walk away from all the naysayers.

- Find hope as you walk with faith-filled friends.

- Find hope in partnership: God is with you. You are not alone.

- Find hope in the midst of tragedy by refusing to blame God.

- Find hope when all is lost by acknowledging God's sovereignty.

His banner over us is love,
Our sword the Word of God;
We tread the road the saints above
With shouts of triumph trod.
By faith they, like a whirlwind's breath,
Swept on o'er every field;
The faith by which they conquered death
Is still our shining shield.
Faith is the victory!
Faith is the victory!
Oh, glorious victory,
that overcomes the world.

—John Henry Yates, "Faith Is the Victory"

CHAPTER 6

FAITH, OUR VICTORY

My father was a man of God who pastored for fifty years, planted five churches, and sang in a gospel group called the Freedomaires. He lived his life fervently for the Lord. By his midfifties, he had developed a weak heart resulting from three major heart attacks. The doctors told us to prepare for his funeral. However, he lived thirty more years after that death sentence. Dad's last heart attack occurred while he was working on some projects in his basement. Daddy lay on the floor for hours, too weak to call out for my mother's help. His heartbeat had dropped to eighteen beats per minute, and in that time of great need, he called on the name of the Lord. He asked God to help him, and he told the Lord he was not quite ready to go yet. To some, that may sound like foolishness; but to my father, who had lived a life of faith, it was his best and only option. The paramedics were called when my mother found dad, and they thought he would not see morning. However, through faith, my father defied the natural laws and relied on the supernatural, sustaining power of God. He asked God for an extended life, and he received it.

Later on, Dad was called to the VA Hospital in Virginia, where a team of doctors interviewed him. They were tremendously curious about how he had defied his dire medical prognosis. How was it that he was still alive? His heart rate had dropped so significantly during his last heart attack that his internal organs had begun to shut down. The team of physicians asked him how this was possible, and my father's reply was quite simple: "I believe in taking my vitamins, and I believe in the power of prayer." His faith in God and his belief in the power of prayer were real, genuine, and life-saving.

> NUGGETS OF WISDOM: Now faith is the assurance of things hoped for, the conviction of things not seen. (Hebrews 11:1)

How do you build faith in the face of such overwhelming difficulties

- when you are sick,
- when you are broke,
- when you are divorced,
- when you are in utter darkness,
- when you are . . .

How do you look at the Word of God and step into faith mode when your body or everything around you is screaming something completely different? How do you have hope when it's been ripped away from you? How do you begin to even think that there could be a different outcome than the one that has been pronounced over you?

Faith is *believing* that something good will happen, and that belief becomes the substance of things hoped for. The act of fear is *believing* something bad will happen, and the belief becomes the substance of what is expected. They are both actions based on belief. Therefore, the question arises, Do you have faith or do you walk in fear?

Depending on the Bible translation, there are 365 verses that mention that believers are not to fear. The very thing you fear will come upon you. While things can occur because of something we do, they can also occur because of something we believe. If one believes bad things are going to happen, most assuredly they will. As a result, a self-pronounced curse finds its way in through a skewed thought process that stands in opposition to the Word of God. A perfect example of this is if damaging words are pronounced over a child as he is developing a sense of self. Offensive and demeaning words can determine a belief system that becomes a stronghold in that child's mind, no matter how erroneous.

SHAREWORTHY

What was once foolishness to us [a crucified God] becomes our wisdom and our power and our boast. Life is wasted if we do not grasp the glory of the cross, cherish it for the treasure that it is, and cleave to it as the highest price of every pleasure and the deepest comfort in every pain.

—*John Piper*

Defining Faith

Your faith will define you. It will define your innermost thoughts, and it will determine who you really are or are not. Abraham believed God, and it was accredited to him as righteousness (see Genesis 15:6). What does that mean? It means that God looked at Abraham and called him *righteous* because he simply believed what God said was true. Abraham believed God. The Word of God reads that Abraham, when God told him he would be father of nations, did not waiver in unbelief but grew strong in faith, giving glory to God. Abraham believed and gave glory to God long before he ever saw the promise come to fruition. We can learn from Abraham's life's story. We can take God at His Word. We, too, can believe Him. We can believe in His promises. We can redefine our own life and put our unbelief behind us.

NUGGETS OF WISDOM: "Now the poor man died and was carried away by the angels to Abraham's bosom; and the rich man also died and was buried. In Hades he lifted up his eyes, being in torment, and saw Abraham far away and Lazarus in his bosom. And he cried out and said, 'Father Abraham, have mercy on me, and send Lazarus so that he may dip the tip of his finger in water and cool off my tongue, for I am in agony in this flame.' But Abraham said, 'Child, remember that during your life you received your good things, and likewise Lazarus bad things; but now he is being comforted here, and you are in agony.'" (Luke 16:22-25)

In Luke 16:19-31, there is a parable where a man was defined by his belief. Read the account and think about the person with whom you most identify: the rich man or Lazarus (the beggar who had defining faith). This parable teaches us that even in times of great need, sickness, and death, Lazarus held on to his faith, and so can we. It teaches us that even though we believe, life doesn't always turn out the way we want it. This passage teaches us that even though we suffer here on earth, we will have great relief and reward in heaven. Hang on. There are better days ahead.

SHAREWORTHY

Your beliefs define your life. Your beliefs will define your death. Your beliefs will define everything in between.

—*Robin Bertram*

On the other hand, the rich man did not have a faith that defined his life, but his faithlessness defined his death. We learn through this parable the outcome of the faithless—eternal damnation—and once we reach either side, there will be no crossing over. It teaches us that there is a time to turn and that there is a point of no return. The rich man in the story asked for the impossible. He asked for the dead Lazarus to be able to go back and warn his family. The response: if they did not believe Moses and the prophets, then they would not believe Lazarus either. It was simply too late.

What if I believe and die anyway? If so, you are still victorious. "All these died in faith, without receiving the promises, but having seen them and having welcomed them from a distance, and having confessed that they were strangers and exiles on the earth" (Hebrews 11:13). We can live in faith. We can die in faith. Faith is our victory, either way. Without faith, no man will see the Lord.

NUGGETS OF WISDOM: So faith comes from hearing, and hearing by the word of Christ.

(Romans 10:17)

Building Faith

Faith doesn't just happen. Yes, we are all given a measure of faith, but it is up to us to grow in faith. So how do we grow in faith? Here is your answer: Hear. Believe. Obey. Does that sound too simple? It's not. It is a spiritual principle with legs. Faith is a moving, growing, maturing, advancing practice when you decide to be dedicated to hearing the Word of God. During my time of darkness, I would listen to the Bible on my cell phone. Other days I would turn on the radio and listen to some of my favorite preachers. Did my faith grow? You bet it did. The Word above is true. Are you the kind of person who just shows up to church on Sundays and the rest of the week you are devoid of the things of God? Do you have time daily in your Bible and prayer? Do you go to Bible studies and try to have greater understanding of Scripture? There is no better time than right now.

SHAREWORTHY

Let God's promises shine on your problems.
—*Corrie ten Boom*

NUGGETS OF WISDOM: For in [the gospel] the righteousness of God is revealed from faith to faith; as it is written, "But the righteous man shall live by faith." (Romans 1:17)

Living by Faith

Faith is building, living, and walking in truth. How do we live by faith? We cannot just hear the Word. We have to live the Word. We trust God in our day-to-day existence and make decisions in our thoughts and actions that are based on the Word of God.

We used to live in the rolling hills of North Carolina—in farm country. It was a beautiful place to live. My son was preparing to go to the University of North Carolina for freshman year, and we decided to take a trip to Richmond, Virginia, to shop for school. I had been in prayer that morning when I heard a small whisper in my heart. *You are going to have trouble on the road today. That's odd,* I thought. We all got in the car to make the trip, and I turned to my husband and said, "The Lord said we were going to have trouble on the road today." I knew that was not something that I just came up with on my own. I turned to my son, Logan, and repeated what I knew for sure I had heard during my prayers. I asked my husband to lead us in prayer for safety on the road. You may ask yourself, "Well, why didn't you just stay home?" The answer is simple. I did not hear,

"Stay home today." We prayed and then made the two-and-a-half-hour trip to Richmond. No problem.

We shopped most of the day and then headed back. We were an hour away from home when a massive storm suddenly arose. Everything went black. I felt like I was driving in outer space. I couldn't even see the lines on the road to pull over. My husband yelled, "Don't stop! Just keep going straight!" A tractor trailer flew by, missing us by what seemed like inches. He was so close we felt the car sway to the right as he passed. We drove a few hundred feet or so, then the bottom of our car smacked the pavement, bounced back up, and then smacked again with a loud thumping noise. It felt as though we had lost our wheels. The car swerved in the road, and finally I could see enough to pull over to the shoulder. We jumped out, and as we did, another truck came fishtailing right at our car. Along the shoulder were ten or more cars, all with the right front and back tires flattened. The highway had been in repair and gravel put down where the pavement had been torn up, but the torrential rain had washed away all the gravel. The hole was approximately a foot deep across both lanes on the highway. Needless to say, it was a temporary and inadequate fix. I am convinced had we not prayed before leaving our home, we would have been dead or severely injured.

Through that incident I learned several very important lessons. First, when God speaks, always listen and obey. Second, go with what you feel when you hear that still, small voice. Third, share what you hear with someone so that they can join you in prayer and increase in their own faith. Fourth, your life might depend on the leadership of the Lord. I don't know about you, but I need to learn to listen, more and more, so that I can live day to day by faith.

SHAREWORTHY

Faith is to believe what you do not see; the reward of this faith is to see what you believe.

—*St. Augustine (attributed)*

Draw Near to God

We can pray all day, but God says in His Word that He will not hear if our hearts are full of iniquity (see Psalm 66:18).

We can call out to God. We can beg Him. We can plead with Him, but He knows our heart. If indeed we are asking for the Creator of the universe, the almighty living God, the one who formed us in our mother's womb, to heal, protect, lead, or guide us, then we must draw near to Him with a clean heart and clean hands. We must draw near Him in faith.

> NUGGETS OF WISDOM: And without faith it is impossible to please Him, for he who comes to God must believe that He is and that He is a rewarder of those who seek Him. (Hebrews 11:6)

Unity of Faith

Faith is powerful, especially when others join in unity to stand in agreement with you. Tragedy, sickness, or loss gives an opportunity for a community to come together as one, with one unified purpose and with one common goal. We need to remind one another that in this battle, which we have all had to deal with, there is faith, hope, and love available during the midst of darkness. This battle is an opportunity for deep spiritual growth together as a family of believers and even community. It is an opportunity to find all those treasures life has to offer us and to know that, yes, we can be survivors and, even more, we can be conquerors. We acknowledge by helping one another that there is hope in the darkness, that we can have faith throughout the battle, and that we can be victorious in the battle regardless of the outcome. Stand together in agreement and it becomes an unstoppable force of faith moving your mountain. Faith means to trust in:

- God's protection
- God's provision
- God's promises
- God's sovereignty
- God's guidance
- God's direction for your life and your death

Fighting by Faith

Faith is a tool for battle, and it must constantly be sharpened. In the midst of a battle, there is usually a hero who emerges. A hero will choose a side and refuse to ride the fence, will make a decision and stand by that decision. The hero will make those decisions based on personal beliefs. Choose life, no matter the circumstances. If you do, you've already won. Choose life instead of giving in to the darkness that is meant to destroy you. In a battle, a hero refuses to be intimidated by the enemy. A hero does not run when things get rough, but stands firm, in the midst of the battle, refusing to be moved by circumstance, knowing that he or she is victorious either way. A true hero looks at and embraces all possibilities legitimately and refuses defeat. It is the fight that spurns us toward a deeper walk of faith.

> NUGGETS OF WISDOM: For whatever is born of God overcomes the world. This is the victory that has overcome the world: your faith.
>
> (1 John 5:4 WEB)

Many battles are won by our faith. Faith is *believing* beyond our circumstances. Faith is *believing* when all odds are against you. It is *believing* when your intellect screams you are wrong. It is the most powerful force one can tap into when walking through the battle. Faith is the assurance of things hoped for. Faith stands in the face of loss, sickness, or disease and simply says, "No, I will not give in. No, I will not give up. No, I will not be defeated. I will win either way."

> NUGGETS OF WISDOM: Fight the good fight of the faith. Take hold of the eternal life to which you were called when you made your good confession in the presence of many witnesses. (1 Timothy 6:12 NIV)

Walking in Faith

Walking in faith implies that there should be a motion forward. Our faith should never be static but instead should be constantly growing and moving. My friends, I have walked on this road personally as well as with numerous individuals, some of whom totally recovered, some of whom moved into remission, and some of whom are no longer with us. During this journey, I discovered there were some commonalities between each and every individual. I realized there comes a time in each individual where a decision is made to fight, to stand, or to give in. Each individual must personally decide how to fight. Each individual must personally decide how long to fight. We are to live by faith, walk by it, stand in it, and pray in faith because it is the building block of our future. It is looking past what the eye can see and determining in your heart that you can be more than a survivor; you can be a conqueror.

> NUGGETS OF WISDOM: Yet in all these things we are more than conquerors through Him who loved us. For I am persuaded that neither death nor life, nor angels nor principalities nor powers, nor things present nor things to come, nor height nor depth, nor any other created thing, shall be able to separate us from the love of God which is in Christ Jesus our Lord. (Romans 8:37-39 NKJV)

SHAREWORTHY

God never said that the journey would be easy, but He did say that the arrival would be worthwhile.

—Max Lucado

Scientifically, studies have proved the importance of mind-set in determining an individual's ultimate outcome. If your goal is healing, then fighting is not an option—it is a requirement. It is in faith where the battle is won. We must face our own life and death in faith, reaching out in prayer, and trusting God in the process, therefore living and dying in that faith. The journey requires faith and hope that only God can give.

> NUGGETS OF WISDOM: He said to them, "Because of the littleness of your faith; for truly I say to you, if you have faith the size of a mustard seed, you will say to this mountain, 'Move from here to there,' and it will move; and nothing will be impossible to you." (Matthew 17:20)

Several years ago, a friend who was dying asked me to read the healing Scriptures to him. This was just a week or so before he went on to be with the Lord. After I read to him, we praised God for those words of truth. We celebrated those words of truth. Those healing Scriptures offered hope for that individual until his last breath. They offered comfort in the face of the storm. They offered peace in the midst of a great battle. Heroes of the faith did not receive the promise due them because something else better awaited them. Ultimately, our full physical healing awaits us in heaven.

Refined in Faith

God will refine us through our trials and tribulations. There is no greater place for finding those treasures that add value, meaning, and purpose to our lives than in the midst of such tremendous life-altering struggles. We then can choose not to miss the treasures that lie before us. We, through our trials, are refined like a precious jewel. We are refined like a diamond in the rough. We are refined like a sparkling ruby and smoothed like a beautiful pearl. We are refined in our demeanor, our character, and our attitudes. The small things in life do not move us anymore. Mundane tasks begin to offer us greater joy. We celebrate the small achievements and victories. We take pleasure in and appreciate the wind's movement, the crashing ocean waves, the falling rain on a tin roof, a sunny day, or the scent of a single rose. Life takes on a new meaning. It takes on a new direction. It takes on a new focus when we are faced with life-altering battles.

Rejoicing in Faith

Faith is the impetus for our will to be renewed, our hearts refined, and our spirit strengthened to rejoice through our circumstances. Remember my friend Jack? The last thing Jack wanted me to do was to be sure that his funeral would be a homecoming party. Jack sought a homeland. He was a foreigner and alien in this land; a homecoming party is what Jack asked for, and a homecoming party is what he had.

You see, the Lord rejoices when His servants come home. You and I may not feel like celebrating the death of a loved one, but in Christ we can decide to celebrate for a saint going home to be with the Lord. We can celebrate that he or she is no longer held captive by a body ravaged with pain. We can celebrate that they are no longer fighting to accomplish the day-to-day necessities such as eating, drinking, or sleeping. We can celebrate with our dying loved one that they are growing closer and closer to the Lord each and every day. What do we have to celebrate about? Celebrate that our loved one refused to be a victim to pain, to fear, to terminal illness, or even to death. Celebrate with him that he is now totally free and is in the presence of a Holy God. A true hero finishes his assignment even unto death.

> NUGGETS OF WISDOM: Therefore, since we have so great a cloud of witnesses surrounding us, let us also lay aside every encumbrance and the sin which so easily entangles us, and let us run with endurance the race that is set before us.
>
> (Hebrews 12:1)

I was in Nashville at a National Religious Broadcasters event with Christian Women in Media when I looked up as a man walked by our booth. He was portraying Jesus Christ for the Holy Land Experience in Florida. My heart leaped. For one brief moment, I knew how those who have gone on before me must have felt when their spirit departed from their body. My immediate reaction was to fall on my face in worship to the Lord. During that experience, for just one moment, my heart was filled with indescribable joy. I felt tremendous peace. I felt the overwhelming desire to worship God. I felt the love of God flow over me. For one split second, I felt just a glimmer of what it must be like to be in the presence of Jesus Christ. I believe God allowed that experience to teach me what it will be like when I see His face.

Death for the saint is in that place; it is being in the presence of the mighty God of Creation with a cloud of witnesses surrounding and welcoming home our loved ones. It is a place filled with joy and peace. It is a place where love is ever-present, and in that, we can rejoice and honor our loved ones with a sense of joy, knowing where they truly are. It can be a real homecoming celebration. Treasures await the believer entering the gates of heaven. Faith stands in the face of death and simply says, "God's will be done."

Abide with Me

I fear no foe, with Thee at hand to bless;
Ills have no weight and tears no bitterness.
Where is death's sting? Where, grave, thy victory?
I triumph still if Thou abide with me.
Hold Thou Thy cross before my closing eyes,
Shine through the gloom, and point me to the skies.
Heaven's morning breaks, and earth's vain shadows flee;
In life, in death, O Lord, abide with me!

—Henry F. Lyte

TREASURE CHEST

- Faith will define your life, and it will define your death.

- Faith is our victory, therefore, start from a position of victory.

- Faith is building, living, and walking in truth.

- Faith is powerful, especially when others join in unity to stand in agreement with you.

- Faith is a tool for battle, and it must constantly be sharpened.

- Faith is the impetus for our will to be renewed, our hearts refined, and our spirit strengthened to rejoice through our circumstances.

- Faith stands in the face of death and simply says, "God's will be done."

"Fear not, I am with thee;" Blessed golden ray,
Like a star of glory, Lighting up my way!
Thro' the clouds of midnight, This bright promise shone,
"I will never leave thee, Never will leave thee alone."

—E. E. Hewitt, *"Never Alone"*

CHAPTER 7

FEAR NOT

Two explorers were on a jungle safari when suddenly a ferocious lion jumped in front of them. "Keep calm," the first explorer whispered. "Remember what we read in that book on wild animals? If you stand perfectly still and look the lion in the eye, he will turn and run."

"Sure," replied his companion. "You've read the book, and I've read the book. But has the lion read the book?"

Often we feel that way, don't we? We feel like we know what to do. The question becomes, Will everyone around me know what to do? Then it becomes a question of control. Can I control this situation? Personally, I do not feel safe when I am not in control. What about you? We all want control over our lives, and when we don't have that control, we tend to go into a tailspin.

Liam was a close friend of a friend diagnosed with terminal cancer. He was married with several children. His wife, Atalie, was a stay-at-home mom who knew very little about the business world. When the diagnosis came, Liam felt his life spin out of control. His biggest fear: who would take care of his family? It was a legitimate fear if there is such a thing. He had reason to be concerned. He was the sole support. How would his family survive? Who would provide for them and watch over them?

Gripped by Fear

When I was a young child, my father was building a new home and had laid water pipes in the yard going to the new house. The ditch, which held the pipes, had not been covered because the work was incomplete. My sister and I were running and jumping around the ditch, just playing outside as children do, when I slipped and fell in. My head hit the pipe, and the blow was so hard that the impact knocked me out for just a few seconds. When I opened my eyes, there was a snake crawling over my forehead, and it slithered down my left arm and my side. I looked up, and my sister was standing on the bank screaming so vehemently that my mother thought we were being attacked. Horrified, she ran quickly out to the ditch.

As she looked into the ditch, she saw the snake slithering over me and then away from my body. She also saw another snake, which was a copperhead, only about two feet from my head. My sister pulled me out, and my mother grabbed a hoe and tried to chop the head off the snake. It jumped up to strike at her, missing her only by inches. It then fell back into the ditch, and she slammed the hoe into the dirt, completely severing the head of that snake from its body. I watched the whole episode, and from that day forward, needless to say, fear became a part of me. Fear became my identity.

It took up residency, and I was totally unaware. I embraced it. I thought it was just who I was. It was a faulty identity, being fearful that is, but I allowed it to become my signet ring, forever sealed by its paralyzing grip.

SHAREWORTHY

We can easily forgive a child who is afraid of the dark; the real tragedy of life is when men are afraid of the light.

—*Duane Sommerness*

NUGGETS OF WISDOM: For God has not given us a spirit of timidity, but of power and love and discipline. (2 Timothy 1:7)

Spiraling Out of Control

Fear causes us to want to be totally in control, but God wants us to be okay with not being in control. He wants us to allow Him to be in control. That incident later wreaked havoc in my life and caused me to spiral out of control because I never properly dealt with the fear.

When your life is spiraling out of control, you really have no choice but to grab God's hand and let Him guide you to your final destination. When you are up against a brick wall, with few or no options, you have to trust God. He determines life and He determines death. He determines everything in between. Trust me, the first emotion you will feel when difficult days come, when you get a bad diagnosis, or you experience loss or tragedy is fear. You will be overwhelmed at first. I was.

When I was first told that I could have a potentially fatal disease with no possibility of recovery, I became so confused that I could hardly function. Small tasks were almost too much to handle. If you are like me, your thoughts will be jumbled and your words incoherent. Your brain can't rest. You will be tempted to entertain every thought that comes into your mind, but that is a trick of the enemy. You will have to take yourself out of panic mode.

> NUGGETS OF WISDOM: Have I not commanded you? Be strong and courageous! Do not tremble or be dismayed, for the LORD your God is with you wherever you go. (Joshua 1:9)

Fight Fear with Faith

Fear immobilizes and paralyzes us. Fear leads us into sin and away from faith. It causes various physical and emotional issues, or it complicates the ones we have. It brings confusion, causes us to hide, and keeps us from serving God. Fear causes us to flee when we should stand firm.

> NUGGETS OF WISDOM: Do not fear, for I am with you. Do not be afraid, for I am your God. I will give you strength, and for sure I will help you. Yes, I will hold you up with My right hand that is right and good. (Isaiah 41:10 NLV)

Take a Scripture like the one above and remind yourself daily that God will help you. He will strengthen you. He will uphold you. He is with you. You may ask yourself, "How do I refuse to be fearful?" You stand first on Isaiah 41:10, knowing that God is with you, knowing that He is your Guide, your Authority, your Provider, your Protector, and your Comforter. Listen to the Word of God. Faith comes by hearing the Word of God. We are all given a measure of faith. Start there. To build your faith, you have to hear . . . you have to be proactive and listen.

Sickness, like fear, can become your identity. I decided early on that I would have to fight fear, and later I decided I would fight sickness. Have you ever heard someone say, "My cancer is . . ." First of all, do not claim it as yours. Why take ownership of a disease? Sickness is an enemy, as well. God did not give us fear or sickness. Why acknowledge that it belongs to you or is a part of you? Instead, why not choose to declare it an enemy with whom you refuse to associate? I know, that may sound a little strange, but in doing so, you are, in a sense, refusing to give in to the illness. You are choosing to reject ownership, thus declaring it an unwanted invader. Fighting fear and fighting sickness with faith are decisions only you can make in order to prevent them from defining the days of life left on this side of heaven. Practice walking in faith at the very core of your being, and fight the enemy of your soul.

NUGGETS OF WISDOM: Yes, even if I walk through the valley of the shadow of death, I will not be afraid of anything, because You are with me. You have a walking stick with which to guide and one with which to help. These comfort me.

(Psalm 23:4 NLV)

A rod is used symbolically here as a tool used by a shepherd to protect, direct, and lead his sheep. God will protect, direct, and lead you during the time of trouble. The staff is symbolically used in reference to the authority of God. God is the ruling authority over all things—in our living and our dying and everything in between. Have faith in God's protection, His provision, His promises, His sovereignty, His guidance, and His direction for your life. He has the solutions.

SHAREWORTHY

What is fear but an emotion? Wrong. It is a ruler, never being satisfied with just taking up space; it demands homage.

—*Robin Bertram*

Oftentimes as a young woman, I would make excuses for not wanting to try new things. I would avoid uncomfortable situations. Behind much of my decision-making lurked a spirit of fear. It had become a greater dominating force every time I bowed to its wishes. It was not until my early thirties, and after the birth of my two children, that the fear I had given access into my life through that childhood tragedy tried to rule me. Fear took on an even greater presence.

It was no longer happy hanging in the shadows. It wanted a voice. I started having severe panic attacks. The childhood trauma created a path of insecurity, trying to destroy everything I was created to do. It literally took two decades of my life to finally come to the understanding that fear was going to destroy me if I did not destroy it. To begin, you have to identify the enemy of fear.

> NUGGETS OF WISDOM: Be of sober spirit, be on the alert. Your adversary, the devil, prowls around like a roaring lion, seeking someone to devour.
> (1 Peter 5:8)

Fight Fear by Identifying the Enemy

The Bible tells us that people perish for lack of knowledge. I was ignorant about the importance of resisting fear. Fear is simply a tool used by the enemy to kill, steal, and destroy your plans for a future. God has said that no matter what we might be facing in life, "Do not fear."

The more you fear, the more you become susceptible to it. It is your enemy because it causes you to lose focus on the reality that God is really in control. Do not walk in agreement with it. It is not of God, and He did not give it to you. Franklin D. Roosevelt once said, "The only thing we have to fear is fear itself." Fear is the real enemy; fight it with everything in you.

> NUGGETS OF WISDOM: There is no fear in love, but perfect love casts out fear; for fear has to

do with punishment, and whoever fears has not
reached perfection in love. (1 John 4:18 NRSV)

Fight Fear with Love

Perfect love combats the fear in your life. Perfect love, which
emanates from God, through God, and in God, is our defense
against fear. As you meditate on the Scripture above, remember and
trust that God is not punishing you through this time of darkness.
Believe that. Accept that. Stand on that. There is a real mental battle
that says, *I must have done something* or *Why are you punishing me,
God?* Erase those thoughts. Replace those thoughts. God loves you,
He created you, and He is for you. Perfect love does not induce punishment . . . discipline, yes, but punishment, no. God is a loving God
who wants you to have an abundant life.

You are not being punished.
You are not being punished.
You are not being punished.
Perfect love casts out fear.

Perfect love comes from God, through God, and is God; therefore, in order to fight fear, our strong defense is learning to walk in the
love of God. We understand that God loves us. We understand that
He gave His Son for us that we might have eternal life if we accept
Jesus as our Lord and our Savior. We understand that He fights our
battles for us. We understand that it is His will for us to have life and
life more abundantly. If we can keep that at the core of our thoughts,

we will have a tool to fight the enemy of our souls that torments our minds during such challenging times. Take fear captive and cast it out. Remember, when we are being tormented with fear, it is not of God or from God, but from the devil (see Romans 8:15). Let the love of God wash over you. Cry out to Him today. Let His light and love flood your soul and give you peace, and that alone will drive out the enemy of your soul.

SHAREWORTHY

Perfect love, which emanates from God, through God, and in God, is our defense against fear.

—Robin Bertram

NUGGETS OF WISDOM: For you have not received a spirit of slavery leading to fear again, but you have received a spirit of adoption as sons by which we cry out, "Abba! Father!" (Romans 8:15)

Fight Fear with Facts

The Statistic Brain Research Institute reports that 88 percent of the US population is fearful of health-related issues that will never happen, 68 percent of the US population has a fear of death, and 60 percent of the population is fearful about things in general that will never happen. The University of Minnesota reports a correlation between chronic fear and health. "Fear weakens our immune system and can cause cardiovascular damage, gastrointestinal problems such as ulcers and irritable bowel syndrome, and decreased fertility. It can lead to accelerated aging and even premature death."[1]

Fear is a God-given emotion to alert one that they are in some kind of danger, but it can become something much more. It can be a tool the devil will use against you. Have you heard the acronym for fear: *f*alse *e*vidence *a*ppearing *r*eal? The devil is a trickster. He is so cunning that he can make you believe horrible things are going to happen even when they are not. He whispers the very worst scenario and convinces you that things will be that way. Fighting fear based on facts, not feelings, is another important step toward working through your struggle, but we need to know where to look for help. Resist the temptation to think of the worst scenario.

SHAREWORTHY

Fear is like a ferocious lion looking for its prey. You cannot give in; it will surely overtake you.

—*Robin Bertram*

NUGGETS OF WISDOM: Praise the Lord, O my soul. And forget none of His acts of kindness. He forgives all my sins. He heals all my diseases. He saves my life from the grave. He crowns me with loving-kindness and pity. (Psalm 103:2-4 NLV)

I had ministered to an elderly man who was fighting terminal cancer, and he would often say, "If I'm healed here or if I'm healed there, either way, I'm healed." Was this man in serious denial? No, he was refusing to give in to fear. He refused to let fear determine his course. He understood that his ultimate healing would come when he was in heaven with Jesus, so through his confession, he was refusing to succumb to the victim mentality and allow fear to dominate his thoughts.

As I said before, the first thing you or a loved one will feel when faced with a traumatic situation, sickness, loss, or terminal illness is fear. Fear comes to visit and then to take up permanent residency. It pops up out of nowhere. You will think and feel thoughts you would have never imagined thinking or feeling before. Fear whispers in your ear. It tells you your worst nightmare over and over and over again. In Scripture we have a clear directive to not worry about tomorrow because today has enough troubles of its own (see Matthew 6:34). Take today. Concentrate on today. Look for the beauty of today. Make a point to look out of your window. Get out if you can. If you can walk, go out for a walk. If you can read, read a good book. If you can talk, talk to a friend or a loved one. Make each and every moment that you have count. Do what you can do. Embrace life. Echo God's words. Enjoy every moment.

Fight Fear with Scripture

The Bible is your treasure trove. Consider for a moment the possibility of taking those negative emotions regarding the situation, throwing them out of your mind, and replacing those emotions with

Scripture that promises you peace, joy, comfort, healing, and longevity. Personally, when several potential diagnoses came and test upon test to prove or disprove the inevitable were administered, I would be lying if I said fear was not an issue. It was. I spent one solid year with no definitive diagnosis and no real answers and a year and a half with real symptoms staring me in the face. Internal struggles, tears, prayers, and begging the Lord took front stage. This became my daily routine. Eventually, I began to replace my thoughts with the Word of God, so I made a list of all the Scriptures related to healing that I could find, and I read them out loud over and over again. You might have a different issue, but the answer to your problem is the same. God's wisdom tells us through His Word to stand in the battle. It tells us to stand in faith or we won't stand at all. It also tells us that God will fight for us.

NUGGETS OF WISDOM: The LORD will fight for you while you keep silent. (Exodus 14:14)

Fight fear with God's precious promises. Stop for a moment and think of all of God's promises: promises of health, healing, and long life. Once you decide in your mind it is true, then you have to learn how to stand on those promises. You can choose to be the exception to the rule. You can choose to declare the promises of God, stand firm, and do not back down. You can choose to use your spiritual weapons of warfare to fight against the illness: prayer, fasting, worship, and praise.

NUGGETS OF WISDOM: Do not be anxious about anything, but in everything by prayer and supplication with thanksgiving let your requests be made known to God. (Philippians 4:6 ESV)

Fight Fear with Prayer

Pray.

Pray.

Pray. But do so from a position of victory.

Your victory has already been won—God knows your future. He knew your end from the beginning. You are in His loving hands. Fear is a tool of the enemy to get your eyes off of God or any productive attitude you might otherwise have. Ask the Lord to forgive you for participating in works of the flesh and works of darkness. Now thank God in faith, believing you have received, and watch the King of Glory move on your behalf.

Prayer is the answer for bringing about change. Prayer is the process by which change is instigated. It brings us into communion with God, the Father. As we spend time in His presence, we desire to become more like Him. We begin to see ourselves as He created us. We apply the knowledge obtained through His written Word, reflecting His divine character and nature, and we become transformed into His glorious image. This process is, without doubt, the fundamental path to healing and restoration of a broken body or spirit. Dr. E. Stanley Jones, a twentieth-century Methodist Christian missionary and theologian writes, "'We do not know why it is that the worriers die sooner than the nonworriers, but that is a fact.' But I, who am simple of mind, think I know;

we are inwardly constructed, in nerve and tissue and brain cell and soul, for faith and not for fear. God made us that way. . . . To live by worry is to live against Reality."[2]

When you give this battle to God, laying down your burdens, you receive rest and peace found only in Jesus. Confession is the key to healing and restoration, but it also involves an exchange. Jesus Himself has given an invitation for all who are heavy or oppressed. He invited all who desired rest to take His yoke upon them. After twenty-five years of prayer ministry, I have found that many people are bound by fear, anxiety, and depression. I have also found that many people do not know where to get assistance. There is but one answer, and that is in the written Word of God. You see, for the believer, we have an assurance. For the unbeliever, today is the day of salvation. Believers have a written picture of the glories that await us. We have a promise of no more tears and no more pain. We have a vision of a home prepared for us. We have a vision of a beautiful city. Heaven is real, and for those who believe, it will be their new home.

> NUGGETS OF WISDOM: There is an appointed time for everything. And there is a time for every event under heaven—A time to give birth and a time to die. (Ecclesiastes 3:1-2)

Hidden Treasures

Can you imagine? God calls you His jewels. You are His hidden treasure, and He is our hidden treasure. The world cannot embrace spiritual things. That is left up to those who are spiritual. Jesus Christ, through the power of the Holy Spirit, gives us wisdom that the world does not understand. He gives us peace that the world cannot experience. He gives us understanding that certainly supersedes the wisdom of man. He gives us wisdom on how to fight or stand in this battle even when we feel like we are in utter darkness. He is there leading and guiding us through.

God Is in Control

Remember my friend Liam, who was concerned about his family and who would take care of them? Just a few short years after Liam went to be with Jesus, Atalie, his wife became an entrepreneur. She built a business to support the family and several years later went back to school to become a nurse practitioner. Her children went to college and are very successful in their adult lives. Her community surrounded her precious family, and she had the support she needed.

God is always in control. We are not. As I look back at my life, from the time this little girl fell into that ditch, I clearly understand that God has me in His hand. Accept that God is sovereign and has a plan and purpose for your life. Accept that He protects His children. Renounce fear. Break associations with fearful mind-sets. You can do this. With God's help, the power of the Holy Spirit, and a willing heart, the Lord will strengthen you in the midst of your own battle. You can trust Him with your life, your family, and your future. Embrace Him today, and refuse to miss those beautiful treasures that await you on this side of heaven.

NUGGETS OF WISDOM: "They shall be mine," says Yahweh of Armies, "my own possession in the day that I make, and I will spare them, as a man spares his own son who serves him."

(Malachi 3:17 WEB)

TREASURE CHEST

- Fight fear with faith.
- Fight fear by identifying the enemy. Fear is an enemy not an identity.
- Fight fear with the love of God.
- Fight fear with facts; don't let your mind wander.
- Fight fear with Scriptures . . . list them and meditate on them.
- Fight fear with prayer.
- Fight fear with the certainty of heaven.

Forgiveness—what a joyful gift!
You love me, Father God, as if
I never turned away.
You give what I can never earn—
A favor, Lord, I can't return,
A debt I cannot pay.
Forgiveness—what a joyful sound!
I'll share Your gift with all around,
For none of us can pay.
Forget what others owe to me!
I set us both completely free!
I wipe their wrong away!

—Ken Bible, *"The Joy of Forgiveness"*

CHAPTER 8

HIDDEN TREASURES

Years ago, while in prayer, I felt the Lord impress upon my heart that I was to ask my father to forgive me. I was perplexed. For much of my life, he and I had a good relationship. He was a quiet, calm man who worked hard and cared for his family. He was away from home a great deal of the time because he planted five churches, pastored, sang in a gospel group, and worked a full-time job. The Lord showed me in my prayer time that I had hidden resentment because of his absence from our home. As a child, I did not understand his heart and dedication to the Lord. I only experienced a sense of loss because of the lack of time I had with him as *Daddy*. I sat down and wrote him a letter asking him to forgive me for the resentment I had held in my heart against him. He called after receiving the letter, and our conversation went something like this:

"Will you forgive me, Dad?"

"Robin, I don't understand."

"Daddy, you don't have to. Will you forgive me?"

Then Dad responded in great kindness, "Of course I will."

"Thank you, Daddy, and I am truly sorry for harboring ill will against you in my heart."

God's forgiveness will release you, and now you must also release others.

SHAREWORTHY

No prayers can be heard which do not come
from a forgiving heart.

—*John Charles Ryle*

Forgiveness opens the door for restoration in the relationship. For me, this was one of my greatest treasures. That hidden resentment not only separated me from my dad, it separated me from receiving the love of my heavenly Father. From that time on, our relationship changed. We became best of friends. Oddly enough, this was also a time when I felt as if God was truly my Father—in the deepest sense of the word. I felt God's love, as if a wall had come down and His love came flooding into my soul.

There is a tremendous connection between how we feel about God and how we feel about out natural father. When your natural father lets you down, or worse, abandons or abuses you, it becomes difficult for you to see God clearly. For those struggling with tragedy, loss, or long-term or terminal illness, setting relationships right is of the utmost importance. Some individuals who are terminal will hold onto life until they have the chance to reconcile. My experience with Sam comes to mind.

Sam was a young man who believed his father had refused to come to the hospital when he was born. He held deep-seated anger against him. During one of our prayer sessions with him and his mother, she realized he had believed this lie for many years. When she explained that his father had been in the birthing room during delivery, Sam broke down and cried profusely, letting go of years of anger and disappointment with just a simple prayer.

Take a few minutes, no matter your age, and decide to forgive your father or mother for their shortcomings. You may even need to go to them or write them a letter. When you make this choice to forgive, you are freed from the toxic, emotional baggage you've carried around, and furthermore, you can begin to see God more clearly as the loving, perfect Father that He is. Earthly fathers are meant to reflect God's image. When they fail to reflect God, His character, and His nature, children often become embittered toward not only their earthly father but also their heavenly Father. God wants you to know all the love and benefits He has in store for His children: His covenant promises, His protection, and His provision for your life. Unforgiveness blocks the flow of that love and the benefits that await you.

> NUGGETS OF WISDOM: The secret of the Lord is for those who fear Him. And He will make them know His agreement. (Psalm 25:14 NLV)

It Is a Choice

Forgiveness is a choice, but we are commanded to be peacemakers. For all who desire understanding and discernment, Solomon writes, "If you seek her as silver, And search for her as for hidden treasures" (Proverbs 2:4). Forgiveness is a big part of living, and it is a big part of dying. Forgiveness is a choice not a feeling, and we are to forgive and accept being forgiven. When we do it God's way, we are to go to the offended party and admit we have sinned against them. Not an easy thing to do, but there is such freedom that comes through confession. Saying I'm sorry is not enough. Saying I am sorry does not admit the sin that was committed. Unforgiveness can literally make you sick if you hold on to it long enough.

SHAREWORTHY

Hard hearts become softened when they forgive, and love flows into a once-empty heart, pushing all the bitterness out.

—*Robin Bertram*

NUGGETS OF WISDOM: The spirit of a man can help him through his sickness, but who can carry a broken spirit? (Proverbs 18:14 NLV)

For those who have wronged you, hurt you, or even abused you, you become the victor the moment you decide to forgive them. Now bless them, pray for them, and refuse to repay evil with evil.

How can I bless the one who has created devastation in my life? The answer to this problem is only through the power of God. He sends His precious Spirit to strengthen us. Remember, you can do all things through Christ Jesus who strengthens you. He has already given you the power to be an overcomer, so decide today.

Next, pray for the person. That is the best assurance that you will have God working on the situation, when you choose to do things His way. God will not work on your behalf or in the situation if you take matters into your own hands and become the judge. God is the Judge, and He will not relinquish His responsibility to another. Lastly, never repay evil for evil. God can't intervene in that situation. He won't. If you want and need God to work in the situation, just do it His way and forgive.

> NUGGETS OF WISDOM: For the Lord will not turn away from a man forever. For if He causes sorrow, He will have loving-pity because of His great loving-kindness. He does not want to cause trouble or sorrow for the children of men.
> (Lamentations 3:31-33 NLV)

Forgiveness as Peacemakers

Christians are commanded to be the peacemakers; therefore, it is up to you to take the first steps toward reconciliation. As we reflect Christ in our relationships, we must remember that He never once demanded His "rights." Instead, He graciously forgave others as they sinned against Him while asking us to forgive them also. You want to settle matters quickly in a spirit of humility. The Bible says that a soft answer turns away wrath.

Cynthia, an older woman in her sixties, developed lung cancer and had only a short three months from the time of diagnosis until her death. She was estranged from her family for many years because of poor lifestyle choices, but she became a Christian in her later years. She reached out to her sons to make amends but to no avail. However, on her deathbed, all three sons came to see her. She had the opportunity to tell them she really did love them and that she was sorry for failing them as a mother. One by one, they forgave her. After they left the room, Cynthia reached up, took off her oxygen mask, and said, "I can go home now."

One of my favorite Scriptures found in Proverbs states that when a man's ways please the Lord, He makes even their enemies to be at peace with them (see Proverbs 16:7). You see you may not be great friends with the one who has offended you when there has been a breach in the relationship, and that's okay, but you can certainly be at peace with them. Do what you can do; that's all you are responsible for.

Forgiveness Through Action

How can I forgive? You forgive by choice and through actions. There is a story in Scripture where a father had two sons: one who followed all the rules, the other rebellious and determined to live his life as he pleased (see Luke 15:11-32). The older son stayed with his father, working faithfully by his side, while the younger left home and spent his inheritance. He found himself penniless and willing to eat pig's food. He finally came to his senses and returned home hoping to just be a servant in his father's house. Instead, his father greeted him with open arms, with his best robe for his son, a ring for his finger, and sandals for his feet. He prepared a great celebration. His father's actions clearly give us a picture of a father willing to forgive his son for his folly and a son humbled enough to receive that forgiveness. It is forgiveness in action.

What is your condition today? Do you need to release someone who has disappointed you, greatly hurt you, or even tried to destroy you? My friend, there is a way and it is good. Follow the precepts found in Scripture, and you will be freed. You will be healed in your heart. You will be restored. Do you want to be forgiven of your sins? Then the Bible tells us we must forgive those who have harmed us. How often do we forgive? Jesus gave us the answer: seventy times seven, meaning over and over again.

NUGGETS OF WISDOM: "For if you forgive others for their transgressions, your heavenly Father will also forgive you. But if you do not forgive others, then your Father will not forgive your transgressions." (Matthew 6:14-15)

Horrific acts had been committed against Diane. I watched a precious woman as she decided to forgive her mother and father for allowing an abortion to be performed on her as a young girl because her father had raped her. She spent her life in counseling, and she was on prescription medicine for most of her adult life to help her deal with the pain. All to no avail. She desperately needed to forgive both of them for the atrocities that had been committed against her. As she sat in my office and prayed, she raised her head, hands shaking and tears streaming down her face, and stated, "I choose to forgive." She was set free of years of depression in that very instant. She moved on to become a prayer minister herself after years of suffering.

Forgiveness is a necessary step in all healing: spiritual, emotional, and physical (see Matthew 6:14-15). It is not an option; it is a command. It is a weapon of warfare as it strips away the rights of the devil in tormenting, harassing, and oppressing those who have held onto resentment and bitterness. Hearts that choose to forgive open themselves up to receiving God's merciful hand of restoration. Unforgiveness binds individuals to hurts and pains of the past and locks them into deep-seated anguish. It blocks the flow and prevents receiving of the love of God.

Hidden Sins of the Heart

You've heard the old adage "Time heals all wounds." Well, that may be true in some cases, but for the most part, it isn't. We have to take a proactive stance in our own personal healing and not leave it up to chance. Sometimes we need more than time; we need to address our wounds head-on and deal honestly with the reasons they are still with us.

One morning I prayed and asked God to heal the hidden sins of my heart; this was a sincere prayer and one I had not asked before. I had enough going on in my life at that time to just deal with the issues of the day. However, God had another plan. I was in my kitchen midmorning, and a very painful thought came to mind of an incident of the past. A little later, I had another thought of a very painful comment that was made by a family member years before. It just popped into my head. Then, a third memory of a very deep hurt I experienced in my marriage came to mind. I cried out, "God, what is going on here?" I had not felt so bad in years. He spoke to my heart and said, "Robin, you asked Me for this." Sobbing before the Lord, my knees hit the floor. I begged God to forgive me for the issues I held on to and so carefully covered up. If you are like me, you may want to pray this prayer:

Dear Heavenly Father,

Please expose to me the hidden sins of my own heart. Help me to walk free of all those offenses I have so carefully covered up. Help me to uproot those wicked and ungodly thoughts and feelings and release those I have been angry or bitter toward. Cleanse me today, Father, from all the things I have chosen to hold against others, and I confess these things as sin. In Jesus' name, I pray. Amen.

A Repentant Heart

As stated earlier, forgiveness is a decision not a feeling. Once the decision is made, restoration will begin. Make no mistake, God will never hold you accountable for another man's sin, but He will hold you accountable for not forgiving that individual for their sin against you. Scripture is very clear on this principle. Each individual has personal responsibility for his own actions; therefore, you should repent. God is a just God, and the one who sins will bear the punishment of that sin. And please remember, forgiveness is an act more for your own benefit than for the benefit of the offender. It releases you from the effects of the sinful act committed against you. A repentant heart is emancipated from the past, and divine forgiveness washes away that sin; it is then forgotten in the mind of God. It starts with a simple decision to forgive others who now need your forgiveness.

SHAREWORTHY

God pardons like a mother, who kisses the offense into everlasting forgetfulness.
—*Henry Ward Beecher*

NUGGETS OF WISDOM: Bear with each other and forgive whatever grievances you may have against one another. Forgive as the Lord forgave you.
(Colossians 3:13 NIV)

An Unwilling Heart

A friend, Casey, received a call out of the blue. She was estranged from her family for many years. She made decisions early on in her life that her family did not agree with, so they cut her off and had no communication with her. Her father was sick to the point of death and reached out to her. She rushed to his bedside several states away. When she got to the hospital, she had some private time with her father. The next morning her mother strongly suggested that she "get on the road" and not waste any time. Later Casey called to check on her father only to have her mother hang up on her. Why this story? The pain of unforgiveness runs like a deep river. It is almost impossible to turn in another direction, but with God, all things are possible. I remember her saying through her tears, "What did I ever do that was so bad? Why can't they just forgive me?"

Sadly, her father did pass away, but thankfully only after she had the opportunity to spend some time with him and let him know how much she loved and treasured him. Those few hours before his death were priceless to her. How tragic, though, that a family was literally torn apart because of stubborn hearts that were too proud to just let go.

In times of such difficulty as facing illness or death, forgiveness is a treasure that cannot be underestimated. It is a necessary element for the one struggling with an illness of any kind. It's essential to both their emotional and spiritual well-being. What can you do? Make it right. Forgiveness allows your heart to feel joy again when you release your offender. Encourage forgiveness. Lead the family in forgiveness.

NUGGETS OF WISDOM: A brother who has been hurt in his spirit is harder to be won than a strong city, and arguing is like the iron gates of a king's house. (Proverbs 18:19 NLV)

Make Peace with the Past

Those who are sick or facing terminal illness must come to grips with things from their past that they cannot change. Most often they feel that they haven't been given adequate time to really deal with difficult issues. I know. That's how I felt. Encourage yourself or your loved one. Here are some actions steps that will help you make peace with your past:

- Acknowledge past mistakes and forgive yourself.
- Do not deny your emotions but accept and release them.
- Refuse to punish yourself for mistakes.
- Learn from your past mistakes.
- Make things right with others.
- Apologize. Tell the truth.
- Accept what happened, and avoid blaming others for the outcome.
- Grieve your regrets with an end in sight and then declare no more grief over that issue.

NUGGETS OF WISDOM: For the sorrow that is according to the will of God produces a repentance without regret, leading to salvation, but the sorrow of the world produces death. (2 Corinthians 7:10)

Let Go of Regrets

Most people regret missed opportunities, what they did *not* do, more than regretting things that they *did* do. Regret can be toxic.

In my past experiences in prayer ministry, as I walked with families who had loved ones facing terminal illness, I noticed that it was common for some members of the family to experience deep regret. "Why didn't I say . . .?" "Why didn't I spend more time . . .?" "Why didn't I help out more?" "Why didn't I make it right?"

Here are some tips to help minimize the potential for regret for the family of those facing long-term illness:

- Organize a list of friends who will take one day a week to help out.
- Help family members settle disputes from the past.
- Extend forgiveness.
- Encourage family and friends to spend as much time together without it being a burden.
- Help the immediate family as much as possible, even in the small things: cut the grass, go to the grocery store, go to doctor's office visits, send uplifting notes, clean the house, cook meals, visit, make phone calls, and pray.
- Pray often for the sick or terminally ill. Pray in faith. Pray the way they ask you to pray. Do not assume to know how they want you to pray. Ask them.
- Spend time with them and give their caregiver a break to be refreshed and rejuvenated.
- Invite your pastors, as well as prayer ministers, with whom your loved one feels comfortable. Prayer is a powerful tool in such a time.
- Be present and available.

Being Present

Painful memories linger in my mind of a dying man who lost all contact with loved ones until his final weeks and days. His family just could not handle seeing this man, who was so vigorous most of his life, become weak and frail. What a tragic situation. He needed his family, friends, and loved ones to surround him for the long haul. He needed his friends and family during the numerous visits to the doctor or hospital, when he was too tired to go to the grocery store, or simply when he struggled with day-to-day issues. He needed his loved ones to be an even greater part of his life. What could have potentially changed this situation? An open conversation could have brought clarity and understanding instead of misconceptions and pain. Don't be afraid of awkward or uncomfortable communication. Talk it out.

I remember one dear friend who cried out, "Does my son even love me?" He did, of course, but the father questioned this love because the son seemed too busy to visit. As it turned out, it was not busyness keeping him away but, rather, the fear of seeing his father suffering and facing death. I saw a dear man suffer without the visible acts of the love of his children until the last weeks of his life. It may have been out of fear, or denial, or whatever they were personally dealing with, but the pain was real and evident of a dying father. Make a point to be there.

Encourage touch. For the sick or dying, touch is very important. Often, visitors are afraid to touch the dying because of their fragile state of being. However, touch and warmth are important treasures on this side of heaven for the dear ones leaving. A gentle kiss or delicate touch of the hand lets them know that it will all be okay somehow. It lets them know they are loved and cared for. Be generous with touch.

Encourage laughter. We sometimes falsely assume that those who are sick do not want to laugh. This fallacy is usually far from the truth. Often, those who are in such a dire need look forward to the opportunity to laugh, to smile, and to be surrounded with happiness. Share in this precious time and treasure the moments of joy with which the Lord has blessed you and your loved ones. Encourage letting go of the past. Forgiveness is one of life's greatest treasures.

A Willing Heart

On my father's deathbed, he said, "I have no regrets." I thought, *Certainly he must have done something that he regretted.* It took me several years to understand that statement. Dad had no regrets because he lived a life dedicated to God, tried to do the best he could for his wife and children, completed the assignments that God had given him, put God first in his life, and was quick to forgive and ask for forgiveness. I do not know about you, but I hope I can say the same thing.

How do we come to the end of life's journey without regret—not looking back but willing to move forward? How do we go through life without holding on to bitter offenses? There are some things that we can trust in. As believers, God is directing our steps. Nothing can happen to us outside of God's providential will; therefore, we can have the confidence in knowing that God will complete in us the work that He began. We can also trust that He knew the end from the beginning, is not taken by surprise, and is going to lead us through difficult waters to the beautiful gates of heaven.

> NUGGETS OF WISDOM: This is God, our God forever and ever.He will show us the way until death. (Psalm 48:14 NLV)

TREASURE CHEST

- Forgiveness releases you, and you must also release others.

- Forgiveness opens the door for restoration in the relationship.

- Forgiveness is a choice, but we are commanded to be peacemakers.

- Forgiveness allows your heart to feel joy again when you release your offender.

- Forgiveness is a commandment and requires a willing heart.

- Forgive so that you will be forgiven, and refuse to blame others.

- Forgive yourself, and refuse to live a lifetime of regret.

And I feel it in the mornin' dew.
It makes the grass look just like new.
I see it touch a heart full of pain.
And when I look around to see
My Sweet LORD, then it comes to me
Your love is just like diamonds in the rain.

—*Mander McPherson,*
"Diamonds in the Rain"

CHAPTER 9

Diamonds in the Rain

I had a speaking engagement on a cruise to the Bahamas, so my husband decided to go along because it was around our thirtieth wedding anniversary. On one of our island excursions, he wanted to go into a jewelry store and look around. To my surprise, he decided to purchase a beautiful ring in celebration of our anniversary. We started looking at tanzanite stones.

Hidden Stones

The tanzanite stone was discovered in northern Tanzania in 1967. Scientifically called "blue zoisite," the gemstone was renamed as tanzanite by Tiffany & Co.[1] The stone must be heat-treated to remove the brown or burgundy color that is often reflected in it. The heat treatment produces a stronger purplish-blue color and makes the stone *dichroic*, which means it reflects only two colors—in this case, blue and violet. I found the most beautiful blue sparkling stone, but it didn't look that way when it was hidden in the dirt. It had to be unearthed first in order to find its potential beauty. The heat helped

145

to remove the unwanted inclusions that dulled it and also to bring out the stone's brilliance. This is precisely what God does for us. He allows the trials and tribulations of life to refine us by removing all the impurities so that we will reflect His perfect image.

We all have to make a decision to surrender our will to His will as we walk toward heaven. The Bible says that it rains on the just and the unjust. With Jesus by our side, we can get through these storms when we truly decide to let Him lead the way. Tragedy, loss, sickness, or death comes to everyone at some point in life, and when it does, we will definitely begin to figure out what our greatest treasures are in a deep and profound way. It's at these times of great pain that we ask questions about who we are and who God is to us.

We ask questions about our life: "Why do the young have to die?" "Why do the righteous suffer and the wicked seem to flourish?" "Why do I have this illness?" "What did I do so wrong?" "What have I accomplished in my lifetime?"

These questions are common to everyone facing trials, tribulations, disease, and especially death. The answers are easy to find but hard to understand.

Total Surrender

From the viewpoint of a casual observer, my friend Peter seemed to have it all together. He was living the American dream. He was a successful businessman with a loving family, a devoted wife, and twin boys. On the surface, everything was perfect. Peter was in good health and was a respected member of the community.

He had a beautiful home in an upscale neighborhood in Hollywood, California.

One Sunday afternoon all of that changed when he prayed one simple prayer, "God, I surrender." In a relatively short amount of time, the life to which Peter was accustomed was turned completely upside down, and in a matter of months, he found himself out of work, facing divorce, and suicidal. His knees hit the floor, and he cried out to God in utter desperation.

After much soul searching through this time of great darkness, Peter began to see the light. God was working in his heart, and he was rapidly becoming much more than the lukewarm Christian he once was. His life had radically changed, and he was no longer focused on the material goods he could acquire. He came to value what was most important in life: his relationship with God. You see, Peter learned from his experience that life could become very difficult, very quickly, and the things he trusted in were the wrong things. Status and wealth now took a backseat in Peter's life as he totally surrendered to God and found his true treasure. It was in that very dark place that he began to understand who he really was and who God really was to him.

What does it mean to surrender to the Lordship of Christ? We are taught as Christians that we should give our lives to Jesus, but what does that mean? Often, when tragedy, sickness, or loss come our way, we tend to rely on ourselves, our family, the church, doctors, or medicine for our answers and resolution. The truth is that God alone determines our outcome: life and death. God alone is the one upon whom we must rely and to whom we must surrender.

> NUGGETS OF WISDOM: I have been crucified with Christ; and it is no longer I who live, but Christ lives in me; and the life which I now live in the flesh I live by faith in the Son of God, who loved me and gave Himself up for me. (Galatians 2:20)

Jesus gave Himself up for you and me. Now we must give ourselves up for Him. Surrender means to yield ownership. It means to relinquish control over what we consider ours: our heart, our finances, our time, our rights, and even our plans for the future. When we surrender to God, we are simply acknowledging that what we own actually belongs to Him. He is the giver of all good things. We are responsible to care for what God has given us as stewards of His property, but by surrendering to God, we admit that He is ultimately in control of everything, including our present circumstances.

Surrendering to God helps us to let go of whatever holds us back from God's best for our lives. *Surrender* is a term used in battle and implies giving up to the one who conquers. The conqueror is now in control and determines your fate. By surrendering to God, we let go of whatever has kept us from wanting God's ways above our wants.

Jesus Christ, Son of God, cried out when facing His own demise: "Abba! Father! All things are possible for You; remove this cup from Me; yet not what I will, but what You will" (Mark 14:36).

Empty Yet Full

So how can we empty ourselves of our own will? How can we discern what God's will is for our lives? How can we give over our control when we feel like we are falling off a cliff? The answer is found in the opening verses of Romans, chapter twelve. We refuse to be conformed to this world. We renew our minds by the Word of God. We offer our bodies as a living sacrifice. When we empty ourselves, we become full.

> NUGGETS OF WISDOM: Therefore I urge you, brethren, by the mercies of God, to present your bodies a living and holy sacrifice, acceptable to God, which is your spiritual service of worship. And do not be conformed to this world, but be transformed by the renewing of your mind, so that you may prove what the will of God is, that which is good and acceptable and perfect. (Romans 12:1-2)

Here are some valuable nuggets of truth that will give understanding of the will of God. It is His will:

- That no man should perish
- That believers are to be sanctified
- That believers are to produce fruit
- That believers are to make disciples
- That believers are to walk in the Spirit
- That we are to be transformed by the renewing of our minds
- That we are to present our bodies as living sacrifices
- That we are not to be conformed to this world
- That we believe that Jesus is the only way to the Father

- That we are buried with him and will be raised with Him
- That believers are not to seek their own will but His will

To be able to discern God's will for our lives and surrender to Him, we must rid ourselves of worldly thoughts and attitudes, as well as the following:

Surrender

First, surrender your heart to God through Jesus Christ by believing in Him. If you have not given your heart to Jesus, do that today. It's a simple choice. God will do the rest. Believe, confess, and you will be saved. We also have to understand and trust that God has our best interest in mind and He sees the big picture. When we understand this, we can trust Him in everything. He knows what is best for us even when it does not feel like it is best. Remember, God sees the end from the beginning.

Humility

Second, we must humble ourselves and understand our position before God. Jesus, the Son of God, made that decision as He laid aside the entitlements exclusive to a divine God, and we must do the same. It was a choice, a decision of His own making, to refuse to plead for the fulfillment of His own personal safety over the divine will of His Father. Although Jesus had at His disposal the ability to radically change His situation at any time, He chose not to do so. He chose to be obedient even unto death.

> NUGGETS OF WISDOM: Who, although He existed in the form of God, did not regard equality with God a thing to be grasped, but emptied Himself, taking the form of a bond-servant, and being made in the likeness of men. Being found in appearance as a man, He humbled Himself by becoming obedient to the point of death, even death on a cross. (Philippians 2:6-8)

The Sinful Flesh

Third, we surrender our sinful flesh, which also includes surrendering our will to the written Word of God. Choose to get rid of actions, thoughts, deeds, and attitudes that stand against God's Word. When going through difficult situations that require God's help, you cannot expect Him to move mountains for you when you will not move your own. Sin blocks our prayers and breaks our fellowship with God. Sin produces death in us. That alone is reason enough to rid ourselves of the sins of the flesh. When you walk away from sin, you are, in essence, doing His perfect will.

> NUGGETS OF WISDOM: Then Jesus said to His disciples, "If anyone wishes to come after Me, he must deny himself, and take up his cross and follow Me." (Matthew 16:24)

Deny Yourself

Fourth, we deny self. We not only let go of worldly desires but also surrender our plans for the future, our day-to-day plans, our hopes, our dreams, and our wishes, knowing that God knows best.

What do you love? What do you hold on to? If you had to leave this world tomorrow, what would be the most difficult thing to give up? When we think of denying self, we often think that it applies only to sinful desires. While that is certainly a big part of denial, it also involves denying the things to which you feel entitled. We all feel we are entitled to live a long, healthy, prosperous life. We all feel we are entitled to see our children and grandchildren grow. But the Word of God says no one is guaranteed tomorrow—no one. Therefore, while we may want these things, we do not have the guarantee that we will experience these things.

Can you trust the very God who formed you in your mother's womb? Can you trust the God who spoke the world into existence? Can you trust the God who established the boundaries of the seas and the infinite expanse of the skies? "Jesus said to them, 'My food is to do the will of Him who sent Me and to accomplish His work'" (John 4:34).

The emptying of self is a continuous process, and we have to be willing to open ourselves up to God and allow Him to reveal areas in our lives where we are allowing worldly attitudes, expectations, and desires to rule. That is total surrender.

God will renew our minds. We can trust Him completely because He loves us and wants the best for us. He can see the whole picture, whereas we can see just a small part. As we surrender our lives to Jesus, we will experience more and more of the power of God in our lives. Total surrender. Can we, like Jesus, be willing to say, "Yet not what I will, but what You will" (Mark 14:36)? Jesus won the victory for you over your self-will in the garden of Gethsemane. In the garden, God saw the struggle that

Jesus was going through and sent an angel to strengthen Him. In the same way, God knows our struggle, and He Himself will come to strengthen us. No one wants to deny themselves, but true surrender means doing just that.

> NUGGETS OF WISDOM: The Lord their God will save them on that day as the flock of His people. For they are like the stones of a crown, shining in His land. (Zechariah 9:16 NLV)

Beautiful Reflections

God is glorified through His children as He is reflected in them; and for those who choose to believe, they have salvation, healing, deliverance, and reconciliation, which means they also have the promise of resurrection. Just like that precious stone that was unearthed, we, too, have to go through a refinement process to find out who we are and what we will reflect. We were made to reflect God. When we empty ourselves of us, we can fill ourselves with more of Him.

SHAREWORTHY

Surrender means beautiful reflections of the love of Christ coming forth as we yield to Him through total obedience.

—*Robin Bertram*

> NUGGETS OF WISDOM: I have been crucified with Christ; and it is no longer I who live, but Christ lives in me; and the life which I now live in the flesh I live by faith in the Son of God, who loved me and gave Himself up for me. (Galatians 2:20)

For some, the word *surrender* means giving up. That's not the surrender I am speaking of. You do not have to surrender to an illness or just give in to the circumstances you are facing. Surrendering to God is letting Him manage things. It is letting Him take control of life's issues while trusting Him to make the best decisions. Often, when I need to surrender an area of my life over to the Lord, I will recall times from my past where the Lord moved on my behalf. However, it did not feel as though He were. Let me give you an example.

Take Up the Cross

One day I was praying earnestly for the spiritual gifts. I knew they were all real and I wanted them. I was on my knees and heard the Lord in my heart begin to ask me a series of questions.

Robin, will you give up your friends for Me?

"Yes, Lord, I have and I will."

Robin, will you give up your church for Me?

I paused for a moment and said, "Yes, Lord, if my church is in apostasy, I will give up my church for You."

I thought, *What a strange question*, so I felt justified in placing a stipulation on the question.

Robin, would you be willing to give up your reputation for Me?

"Lord, that is hard, but yes, I would be willing to give up my reputation for You."

Robin, would you give up your life for Me?

"Lord, how can I answer that question? How would I ever know, unless someone held a gun to my head? I don't want to be like Peter and say I will but then won't."

The Lord said, *One day, Robin, you will know.*

Later, I did have to give up friends, and in the sight of many, I lost my reputation. God asked me to walk away from my church because it had become an idol in my heart. I had held several important positions in that church, and those positions had given me a false sense of importance. I had to lay them down. I mourned for three months, but when I had been stripped of everything I loved, my true Love was waiting with open arms. God was there for me. He would answer many of my prayers the same day I prayed them. Doors for ministry swung wide open. His grace was abounding. That day became a defining day for me. I understood that God is totally in control. He does not want a halfhearted follower, but a servant completely sold out, ready to do what He has asked them to do without hesitation or stipulation. Just sold out.

NUGGETS OF WISDOM: Surrender yourself to the LORD, and wait patiently for him. (Psalm 37:7 GW)

That brings me to my next point: God does things on His time schedule. Wait on the Lord. You may not understand the *why*, but be content with not understanding. The Word of God says that His ways are higher than our ways. The Bible says that He has our best interest at heart. It says that He will watch over us and work all things together for those of us who are called according to His purposes. That said, we can pray that God removes sickness from us. I did. We can pray until the very end that the Lord heals us and restores us.

Look at the prayer of Jesus as He was in the garden of Gethsemane. "Take this cup from me." Do you hear His plea? "Take this cup from me." "Take this cup from me." Please God, take this cup. "Not my will, but yours be done" (Luke 22:42 NIV). Herein lies the greatest faith one can ever exhibit. Is it an easy prayer? No, it is not. Jesus, before the foundations of the world were created, was in agreement with God's plan for humanity. Yet, in that place of great pain, He cried out to God, "Take this cup from me." We can pray that prayer, too, without question.

> NUGGETS OF WISDOM: "Abba, Father," he cried out, "everything is possible for you. Please take this cup of suffering away from me. Yet I want your will to be done, not mine." (Mark 14:36 NLT)

Miss Ollie had a story to tell, which is quite different than you might expect when praying for miracles. "Hey, you, come over here, it's time to pray!" Miss Ollie would shout out to me across the church parking lot as she and I would then join hands and hearts. Her body was racked with diabetes, her hands crippled with severe arthritis, and her knees swollen with excess fluid. Pain had become her norm. As we entered into prayer, the heavens opened and the Lord's presence was so strong I could hardly stand. We prayed with all the fervor and zeal we could muster. Week after week, month after month, and then year after year, we would pray with no healing and no miracles to transpire. I would walk away from her car with tears in my eyes and say, "Thank You, Father, for the grace and humility I get to experience through the love this precious woman has in her heart for You."

This is what it's all about: one of God's children reaching out and touching another, and then receiving the blessing while being united. God has the perfect plan. Even in her pain, she did not waiver in her faith or her love for God, and her faith was evident to all who knew her. Sometimes we ask God to take our cup away before realizing that He is actually filling our cup to overflowing with His blessings.

NUGGETS OF WISDOM: "Truly, truly, I say to you, unless a grain of wheat falls into the earth and dies, it remains alone; but if it dies, it bears much fruit. He who loves his life loses it, and he who hates his life in this world will keep it to life eternal. If anyone serves Me, he must follow Me; and where I am, there My servant will be also; if anyone serves Me, the Father will honor him." (John 12:24-26)

Follow Him

We surrender our lives each and every day. We align our actions with His will. We follow Him. Some days we just choose to do things our own way, and that's usually when we get into trouble. If you look back at your own life, I think you will see there were times when God led you to do something a certain way, and it was later evident that His way was the best way. I know, for me, there have been many times when He led me, and I was astounded at the outcome. Conversely, I know without a doubt that there were times when He led and I did not follow, only to find things in a huge mess. God leads us like we are sheep. Sheep do not know which way to go, but they will follow the shepherd because they recognize his voice. Do you recognize the voice of God? Do you hear Him say, "This is the way, now walk in it." If you are hearing, be sure to follow.

NUGGETS OF WISDOM: For I know the plans I have for you, . . . plans to prosper you and not to harm you, plans to give you hope and a future.
(Jeremiah 29:11 NIV)

Diamonds Under Pressure

I was rushing around our home unpacking boxes, directing the movers, organizing closets, and rearranging furniture during our move several years ago, when I noticed that the movers had forgotten to unwrap a bookcase in one of my closets. They had worked very hard. It had been a busy day for all of us, and we were now ready to see things come to a close. The movers were on the way out when I raced after them and reported that one bookcase still had their blanket wrapped around it. I knew that they would need to put it on the moving van with them. A young man in the group responded quickly, "Oh, I will take care of that for you." We walked back to the closet together, and as he was untying the cords, he began to ask questions.

"So, I understand you are an author."

"Yes," I replied. "I have written several books and am currently working on one now."

"What else do you do?" he asked.

"Well, I am also a Christian speaker and I work in Christian media."

He continued probing. He wanted to know about every aspect of my work. A dear friend who was helping us out on the front end of the move had treated this young man with great kindness and respect during the loading effort, and I know it had an impact on the young man.

He continued, "I have read a lot. I have studied Hinduism, Buddhism, studied the Torah. I have an interest in all religions. I like to learn all I can."

"Well, that is all okay," I said. "But Jesus said, I am the Way, the Truth and the Life."

He paused, as if he could not breathe for a moment, and then looked up at me with tears in his eyes. "My life has not gone the way I wanted it to go."

"Are you ready to change?" I asked. "Jesus will do it for you. All you have to do is follow Him."

We continued our conversation a few more moments, and I asked to pray for him. That precious young man said yes to Jesus with just one statement. "Jesus said to him, 'I am the way, and the truth, and the life; no one comes to the Father but through Me'" (John 14:6). This young man just needed the truth. My heart leaped for joy; I was so elated. Total surrender—one more entered into the kingdom of God.

My Surrender

Ken and I celebrated our thirtieth wedding anniversary during that cruise, and many would think it was all smooth sailing. That wasn't the case. We had many years of struggle. We had many disagreements along the way. We had a ton of heartbreak that we had to deal with throughout the years. There were times when I thought for sure I could not go on. But early on in our marriage, I settled in my mind that I would surrender my marriage into the hands of a faithful, loving, and just God. I would do it His way. I decided that my way could not take first place. I decided that God's way would ultimately be best for me, our children, and our family. I decided that if I were going to follow God, I would hold on to the truth of His Word and be obedient to it. He got me through. Did my flesh want to surrender what I thought I was entitled to? No. Was it worth the pain? Yes, it was. I know God in a very intimate way because of it, and I know that God's love for me is like diamonds in the midst of the rain.

NUGGETS OF WISDOM: The world is passing away, and also it lusts; but the one who does the will of God lives forever. (1 John 2:17)

TREASURE CHEST

- Surrender to God because He is in total control; you are not.

- Surrender your flesh and refuse to give in to its desires.

- Surrender your presumptive rights for what God has in store for you.

- Surrender by emptying yourself of your own will: your personal desires, your actions, and even your prayers to His leadership.

- Surrender by denying self, taking up the cross, and following after Him.

- Surrender your future. God is in control, and learn to wait for His timing.

- Surrender your will to His will, and trust that it is best for you.

PART THREE

LOOKING UPWARD

I've found the Pearl of greatest price,
More precious far than gold;
No jewel has been found so bright,
His wealth can ne'er be told.
The rose of Sharon bright and pure,
The fairest from above,
No earthly jewel is so fair,
He's God's own gift of love.

—W. E. Catlin, "I've Found the Pearl
of Great Price"

CHAPTER 10

Pearl of Great Price

Does God love me? Does He understand my pain? Does He even care? I remember thinking these very questions as I cried out to Him in the middle of the night. I vividly remember thinking, *He can't love me. If He did, I wouldn't be in all this pain. A father loves his children, so why would my heavenly Father allow this pain to continue?*

I grew up in the beautiful mountains of Alleghany County, Virginia. My dad had 140 acres on the top of what we called Maddy's Mountain. Daddy came to me before he went to be with Jesus and said, "Robin, I want to give you the best of the land." I was the youngest, and Dad and I had grown very close over the years. There were four children, all of whom would get an equal portion of the land as an inheritance, but my portion had a well on it and was relatively flat. For me, this is a perfect example of the love God has for His children. God wants to give us as an inheritance: the very best of the land. God's love is the ultimate love story.

Father Knows Best

I remember many times when my dad did not give me what I wanted. He knew more than I knew. He knew what was best for me, although at the time it felt as if he was withholding good things from me. For example, there were times when he forbade me from going out with the *wrong type* of friends. "But why, Dad? You don't even know them," I would say. "How can you possibly know that I shouldn't hang around with them?"

There was one particular time when my sister and I were forbidden from going to a rock concert in a city that was about an hour from our home. We went anyway. Needless to say, we got into serious trouble. The family car broke down on the way home, and we were picked up by police and taken to the local jail. Lieutenant Miller, a name I'll never forget, stopped at Dunkin' Donuts and bought us hot chocolate and chili at 2 o'clock in the morning. The policeman called my mother, and she just about had a heart attack. I could hear her yelling to my dad, "Paul, wake up. The girls are in jail!" It's so funny now, but to her, at the time, it wasn't the least bit funny. The policeman asked my mother to come and pick us up, but she promptly refused. She said, "They got themselves into this mess. They can get themselves home." Hard lesson. The good news is that we did make it home. Our friend who was with us called her mother, and with snow and ice on the ground, she came in the middle of that cold, dark night and picked us up. Father God is always watching over us, and He helps us in times of trouble. Sometimes He sends someone, an angel, to help us in our time of need. For my sister and me, it was Lieutenant Miller and our friend's mother.

NUGGETS OF WISDOM: "For God's eyes are upon the ways of a man, and He sees all his steps."
(Job 34:21 NLV)

God Sees

The Word of God tells us that He is watching over us, leading, guiding, and directing our steps. Can you imagine a God who cares enough about you to watch over you, a God who sees what you are going through, a God who knows your sorrows and pain? The God I serve does. He has been intricately involved in my life from the moment I accepted Him as Lord. He has proven over and over to me that He sees.

One day, many years ago, I was praying as I was driving to the grocery store. I even asked the Lord to show me where to park that day. My car was facing the sunrise, and I started to cry out for my family, then our nation, and then Jerusalem. I was overwhelmed with His presence. I said in prayer, "God, if I am pleasing you, please let me know." As I sobbed profusely, a complete stranger walked up, banged on my car window, and motioned for me to roll it down. I did. She reached inside and hugged my neck tightly and whispered in my ear, "God loves you." "I know He does," I replied back to this woman through all my tears. She went on to say that her young teens in the car beside me were watching me. She said, "They want you to have this." She had a little stuffed walrus and gently placed it in my hands. She said, "It's their favorite." She went on say that she had been healed of stage four ovarian cancer and had vowed to honor God for the rest of her life. Oh my, what a glorious day. God sees.

God Hears

How do you know that God loves you? First of all, He sent His Son to die for you and me. He took upon Himself the penalty of our sins. Jesus is that Pearl of Great Price. Most likely, there are people in your life willing to walk with you through this trying time. Take just a moment and think about those around you. Think about the love they have in their heart for you. Think about the things that people do for you. Now thank God that you have those treasures in your life.

My son was attending the University of North Carolina, Chapel Hill, as a journalism major. When he entered his junior year, he decided to move in with some friends against my husband's and my wishes. The guys he wanted to live with were all brilliant students, but they liked to party. My husband, Ken, and I decided we would cover his tuition, but he would have to cover his room and board unless he stayed on campus. Logan went to a party off campus at Christmas and then just disappeared. We had no idea where he had gone. I knew he had moved in with those guys, but we didn't even know where they were or how to find them.

SHAREWORTHY

In the midst of our deepest pain, God is watching to see if we will reach for His abundant promises.

—*Robin Bertram*

My husband and I went on a forty-day fast for our son. By week two I was desperate, and on Sunday morning I cried out to God from the very deepest part of my soul, "God, I don't want my baby boy to die." Ken ran into the bedroom and tried to get me to calm down. "You don't understand. He's in real trouble," I said. I knew it, and so did he.

> NUGGETS OF WISDOM: The Lord said: "I have surely seen the affliction of My people who are in Egypt, and have given heed to their cry because of their taskmasters, for I am aware of their sufferings."
>
> (Exodus 3:7)

God Knows

I got out of bed and got ready for church that next morning. We were attending a large church in Durham, North Carolina. Midway into the sermon, my pastor stopped and said, "Church, you know I do not do this; but someone here today has cried out to God, and you said, 'God, I don't want my baby boy to die.'" He continued, "You have to put him in the river of death and trust God. That's right, the river where Pharaoh had the baby boys thrown in to die." It took my breath away. I was stunned. I looked at my husband, and he looked at me. We broke into tears and cried profusely. I knew what the Lord was saying through my pastor: to trust Him with my son's life and his future. My heart hurt. The message wasn't exactly what I wanted to hear, yet I was so thankful that God heard my cry and answered me that very morning.

What I learned through this ordeal in a very real and personal way: God sees. God hears. God knows. God cares. You may think that my experience was just a strange coincidence. You would be wrong. It was the voice of God bringing me comfort in the deepest, darkest time of my life. God loves us, and He does care. My pastor had no idea that my son was in trouble. He had no idea that I had cried out to God that very morning. He had no idea what my heartfelt supplication was for my precious son. God did. One night my husband and I woke up and felt strongly that we were to go get Logan. After six months missing, we found him living off campus with some unsavory characters who preferred drinking and partying over going to class. My husband went in and said, "Son, I am here to rescue you." My son grabbed his wallet, his clothes, and a duffle bag and said, "Dad, I am ready to come home."

God sees. God hears. God knows. God cares.

NUGGETS OF WISDOM: The Lord has loving-pity on those who fear Him, as a father has loving-pity on his children. For He knows what we are made of. He remembers that we are dust.

(Psalm 103:13-14 NLV)

God Cares

One morning, during my prayer time, I distinctly remember an overwhelming desire to help a man in our church who was suffering from cancer. There was such clarity in the direction. I was to go to the hospital and see him. The trip was about a ten-hour drive. I know it sounds crazy, but I told my husband I was to go, but I told him that I wouldn't unless God showed me clearly that it was His desire and not my own thoughts. Several hours later that very same day, I received a call from my church. They asked me if I would fly up, rent a car, and drive this gentleman home. "Of course, I will," I said. Plans were made. I flew up, rented a car, picked him and his precious wife up, and drove them back home. I remember his testimony of God's goodness in church that next week. He said God sent them an angel. No, it wasn't an angel, just a woman willing to hear the voice of God and obey. It was one of those treasures God provided for us, and we both benefited from the opportunity.

God sees. God hears. God knows. God cares.

A Very Special Party

Years ago I had a woman, Faith, join my ministry team. She had a long history of isolation from her family and only had a few friends at church. Faith had been saved for approximately seven years and wanted to volunteer to do administrative work. As the holidays approached, one of my team members decided to throw a surprise Christmas party for Faith. We decided that we would bring gifts only for her. After dinner, we gathered together in the living room and brought all the gifts in the room and sat them at her feet. With amazement on her face, she asked, "What is this all about?" "We just wanted to bless you, Faith, with a party just for you," I replied. Faith then explained that she had never had a party thrown for her: not a birthday party, not an anniversary party, not a graduation party, not a single party . . . ever. Joy flowed over her entire countenance. I remember the tears that streamed down her face, along with a big smile that lasted the entire night. She knew, for the first time in a very long time, that she was truly loved. Unbeknownst to us at that time, Faith was soon to be diagnosed with terminal disease with only a few months to live. God knew what she needed right then, right there, and several months later she went to be with Jesus.

God sees. God hears. God knows. God cares.

Diamond Mines

Over a hundred years ago, when diamonds were first being mined in Africa, a farmer sold his land and headed out to obtain wealth. He searched for several years for diamond mines but to no avail. He returned home penniless, sick, and depressed and eventually ended up committing suicide. The purchaser of his original piece of farmland later found that the property contained one of the richest, most productive diamond mines in the world.[1]

Sometimes we, like this farmer, miss the treasures that lie before us. We miss the treasures that God sends our way. We choose to ignore the blessings and focus on the deficiencies. My plea to you today is to look for those treasures. Look around. Look for those special moments when God sends an angel your way. Look for those people who have enriched your life, and thank them. Look for the gift of a loving hand reaching out to help, and take that help. Count it as a blessing for you and for them.

NUGGETS OF WISDOM: Take my teaching instead of silver. Take much learning instead of fine gold. For wisdom is better than stones of great worth. All that you may desire cannot compare with her.
(Proverbs 8:10-11 NLV)

Have you ever watched *Antiques Roadshow*? I remember a gentleman who had a collection that included five ornamental cups made from rhinoceros horns. Completely unaware of the true value of the cups, he decided to take them to the show for appraisal. He topped their record for the most valuable find with an appraisal of nearly 1.5 million dollars. The cups were ancient Chinese libation cups, which were used for ceremonial purposes during the seventeenth and eighteenth centuries. His initial investment of approximately five thousand dollars resulted in him becoming a millionaire virtually overnight.[2] The lesson here: do not overlook the treasures in your own backyard.

One Valuable Pearl

The wisdom found in God's Word is a treasure. What can we learn about treasures as we search the Scriptures? One of the parables that Jesus taught addressed this very thing. It is a parable about a merchant who was seeking after pearls. Matthew wrote: "Again, the kingdom of heaven is like a merchant seeking fine pearls, and upon finding one pearl of great value, he went and sold all that he had and bought it" (Matthew 13:45-46).

Pearls are valuable. Their formation starts from a mollusk that has been invaded by a parasite. The mollusk then produces a sac around the parasite, and that sac consists of the soft tissue, which is known as the *nacre*. Nacre layers continue to form throughout the life of the mollusk. It's this material that gives the pearl an iridescent appearance—God's perfect design. Imitation pearls cannot match its feel. Natural pearls are valued based on their rarity, as well as their size, color, and roundness. There is a pearl, the Hope Pearl, found in the British Museum of Natural History, that is famous for being the largest saltwater pearl, weighing 450 carats.[3]

In the parable of the merchant, Jesus taught that the merchant sold all he had because he knew the value of that one beautiful pearl. Jesus and His heavenly kingdom represent the Pearl of Great Price. He is the thing after which we must seek, even at great cost. Upon finding Him, we become part of the kingdom of heaven. The merchant understood the great value. He understood the importance of selling all he had. He understood the very greatest treasure was before him and valued far above any and all things he had in his possession.

> NUGGETS OF WISDOM: I will have much joy in the Lord. My soul will have joy in my God, for He has clothed me with the clothes of His saving power. He has put around me a coat of what is right and good, as a man at his own wedding wears something special on his head, and as a bride makes herself beautiful with stones of great worth. (Isaiah 61:10 NLV)

Salvation is a free gift. There is no amount of money that will cover the cost. Jesus loves you and me so much that He was willing to die for us. We need to understand His value so that we can understand how much He values us. He knows your value. He gave His life on a cross so that you could have eternal life. Sin has a cost. Jesus sacrificed His blood to cover the penalty due for our sins. He sacrificed His life so that we could live eternally with Him in heaven. What a precious treasure to find: Christ, and this grace freely given, is of transcendent value.

Accepting the good things that God sends our way is easy. Our challenge is to receive tragedy with a willing attitude, a teachable spirit, and a trusting heart. What is God teaching you in this moment? How should you respond? Can you trust Him in the midst of your pain? Chance is not part of the equation; nothing comes into our life except through the Lord's permission. Accepting His plan for our lives can be the real answer to our own searching, our own issues, and our own personal inner struggles. There can be beautiful treasures waiting for you from the ashes of your personal loss or tragedy.

Here are some significant suggestions to remember in the time of tragedy, which will make the journey less difficult.

1. Understand that God is ultimately in control.
2. Choose to maintain a positive outlook by accepting the fact that God is truly in control and has your best interest in mind.
3. During tragedy, relationships are often strained, but remember it can be a time where they are also strengthened through the process. God always puts people in our lives

at the right time and for a purpose. Choose to be thankful for those people He places in your life at this time.

4. Despite the bleakness of any situation, hold on tightly to the hope that there is a purpose in your pain.

5. Life is a journey of faith, and you are being led by faith through certain doors. Know that God will guide you out of or through anything He has placed before you.

6. Do something encouraging every day. Build yourself up as you grow through the development of your faith.

7. Surround yourself with uplifting people and with positive influences. It's easier to maintain a positive attitude in a crisis than to develop one as you are faced with one. A negative mind-set is always destructive, but at the point of tragedy, it can be devastating.

8. Look for the little miracles every day, treasures given by God. By developing a habit of seeing the hand of God in the small things in life, we can sharpen our spiritual senses, which will allow us to see more clearly in the midst of tragedy.

9. Understand the power of prayer. Prayer is the key to the journey, and it certainly will play a crucial part in your emotional and spiritual healing. If you do not currently have a prayer life, there's no time like the present to begin. Studies have shown a high correlation between prayer and rate of recovery, whether it is physical, emotional, or spiritual; it is a proven tool for our ultimate healing.

10. Trusting God is essential. People asked my friend who lost her husband, "How are you getting through this so

well?" Her response, "Only by the grace of God and how good His grace has been."

11. Keep a journal of your thoughts and feelings. This can help you deal with the day-to-day issues by acknowledging your deepest feelings.

12. Determine to use your experience to be a blessing to someone else. Faith is built often, by watching another go through tremendous situations with peace in their heart. Share your life and story with others.

How do you know if you have enough faith to survive a situation like these we've discussed? It is nearly impossible to know how strong your faith is until you are forced to depend on it. There are dimensions to our self-understanding and to our realization of what a relationship with God is all about that only emerge as we come face to face with our own doubts, questions, and introspection. It is in that place that we find out who God really is to us and who we really are to God. He is the Pearl of Great Price and He knows your struggles; He's willing to carry them for you if you let Him.

My Hidden Pearl

There was a turning point in the health challenges I was facing. I was expecting to get worse with every passing day. The future looked so grim, but after about a year with no further damage, I knew God was doing something. One day I was driving home from a Bible study that I was leading. My contact lens was really bothering me, and it felt as though it had ripped in my eye. As I glanced in the rearview mirror to check it out, my eye was swollen and very bloodshot. I knew I needed to get home. About the same time, I was passing the church that had prayed for my healing. Time and time again I felt like I should stop and say thank you to the pastor and his team for praying for me.

As I was passing it, I felt the Lord lead me to pull in that particular day, despite the issue with my contact lens. I went in and found the pastor and reminded him of his prayers a year before. "Odd that you should come in today," the pastor commented. He then explained that one of his congregants had passed away from the same issue the year before, the very week I had come in for prayer. That very morning of my visit, he had received a letter from her husband that touched him deeply. Coincidence? I think not. He was very moved. I thanked him and encouraged him to keep on praying. My experience was a testimony to God's goodness through answered prayers. He gently laughed, and said, "Your story will be my sermon Sunday morning."

God sees. God hears. God knows. God cares.

When I was in the middle of my storm, two of my biggest concerns were not being able to walk down the aisle at my daughter's wedding and not being able to hold my first grandchild. I did get to walk down the aisle at her wedding, and I have held my first precious little granddaughter. May God be gracious to you, no matter what your story is or what it might become. May God be gracious to you.

NUGGETS OF WISDOM: I will give you riches hidden in the darkness and things of great worth that are hidden in secret places. (Isaiah 45:3 NLV)

TREASURE BOX

- God hears your cries.

- God sees and knows your needs.

- God understands your pains.

- God will get you out of or through whatever you are dealing with right now.

- God will fight for you if you will allow Him to be in charge.

- God moves in the hearts and situations of those who trust Him.

- God will direct your steps and give you victory regardless the outcome.

This world is not my home I'm just a passin' through
My treasures are laid up Somewhere beyond the blue
The angels beckon me from heaven's open door
And I can't feel at home in this world anymore.

—Traditional, "I Can't Feel
at Home Anymore"

CHAPTER 11

THIS WORLD IS NOT MY HOME

My dear friend was facing death. There was not a lot of time to get things together. She had been estranged from her family for many years, and even before she knew she was ill, her constant prayer was for the restoration of her family. She had told me several times that she would do anything to have her family reconciled, even if it cost her her life. As it turned out, my friend lived only three months from the time of diagnosis. God heard her prayer and granted her request. Her family did finally come together and find reconciliation, and it was before her funeral—truly a treasure from God but not as either of us had planned.

Several members of her family were not believers. Before the funeral, one of her brothers kept drilling us, my ministry partners and I, on our beliefs. We answered his questions in love, explaining to him about the power of Christ that had changed his sister from being an alcoholic to becoming a lovely, alcohol-free, passionate Christian woman. His questioning transitioned to sincere questions about faith, God, and eternal life, ultimately resulting in him giving his heart to God the night before the funeral. He said, "After much introspection, I realized that what you had shared with me was the truth. I can no longer deny it. I feel like a new man." Now that's resurrection power. The dead in spirit are raised to life. The very thing my dear friend had asked God for was accomplished; her brother was saved and her family restored.

Reality

When we are faced with a devastating diagnosis, when our health or even life is being challenged, our attention quickly turns to the deeper questions of life: Who am I? Where am I going? What is my purpose for living? There is no other time in our lives when we will, with great introspection, delve into the meaning of our own existence. We will search for the purpose in our pain. We will search for meaning in our trials. We will search for peace in the midst of our struggle. This time becomes a rich environment for discovering those treasures that add value, meaning, and purpose to our lives. The family reconciliation that was the subject of my friend's most heartfelt prayer was achieved, but only at the time of her death not before it. Her family stood looking at her body in the casket, and the reality of life hit.

Acceptance

There are processes that you naturally go through when you have received a bad report or a fatal diagnosis. It first starts with denial and then anger, bargaining, depression, and finally acceptance. True acceptance can only be based on confidence of life after death. If you are certain that when you leave this world you will still live on in heaven, then you can begin to develop an understanding of the process and what eternity will look like. Acceptance for the believer is different from the acceptance of a nonbeliever. Believers realize that they do not come to an end but instead literally just pass over. Believers realize that when they close their eyes here, they will open their eyes there, and the first one they will see is Jesus. Nonbelievers think they will simply come to their end, but that's not true. They will also continue on but not in heaven with Jesus. Instead, they will face eternal damnation. Once salvation has been solidified in your heart and mind, the next step is having peace. Let's look at what the Bible tells us about the process of dying.

Imperishable

You may have wondered what happens to you when you die. One way to think of it is to consider the body like a seed that is planted in the ground. A seed sown does not come to life until it dies. When the seed germinates, it flourishes and becomes a beautiful plant. Our bodies are similar to that seed: through the process of dying, we will leave this weak body and ultimately receive a glorified body (see 1 Corinthians 15:42-44). Although our bodies are perishable and wear out, when we die we will be given a body that will not wear out. Paul taught that, for the believer, the body is:

- sown in dishonor but raised in glory;
- sown in weakness but raised in power;
- sown as a natural body but raised as a spiritual body.

> NUGGETS OF WISDOM: If there is a natural body, there is also a spiritual body. So also it is written: "The first *man*, Adam, *became a living soul.*" The last Adam became a life-giving spirit. However, the spiritual is not first, but the natural; then the spiritual . . . Just as we have borne the image of the earthy, we will also bear the image of the heavenly. (1 Corinthians 15:44b-46, 49)

Jesus died and arose from the grave. So shall every believer. He walked on the earth. He talked. He ate. He did everything we can do now and even more. Believers will arise, like that planted seed, for eternity, first as a spirit and then with an imperishable, glorified body. What was once mortal becomes immortal. This is the victory over death that we are promised through Christ's death and resurrection. What does all this mean?

- It means at some point we will all face our own mortality.
- It means that there is life after death—eternal life.
- It means that we are simply passing through; this is not our home.
- It means that there is hope for us that our departure from our earthly existence is not the end but a new beginning.

There are three parts of a man: the body, the soul, and the spirit.

- The flesh, which is perishable, must take on the imperishable.

- The natural man must become a spiritual man.
- The soul continues and will be sanctified from all the evil this world has offered.

How can we accomplish this kind of metamorphosis? Through the acknowledgment that Jesus Christ is who He says He is. We become life in Him. The victory we have today is found in Jesus Christ, the one who laid down His life, who died on a cross, and who took upon Himself the penalty due for the sins of the world: your sins and mine alike. Jesus Christ emphatically confirms to us who He was and is as He declares His identity through His own words written within the pages of the Holy Bible. Jesus is revealed as the author of life as He explained to Nicodemus the process of being born again, which is spiritual birth. Jesus proclaimed, "For the bread of God is that which comes down out of heaven, and gives life to the world" (John 6:33). This sign, in the natural, was to confirm in the spiritual that He would sustain us and provide us true bread from heaven with the promise that we will never hunger or thirst again. Have you trusted Him as your sustainer? As you and I face hard times, we can trust in God to get us through.

Trusting When You Do Not Know How

Just recently I was asked to do one-on-one prayer ministry with a dear woman in her forties. As a child, her father had repeatedly raped her. Not only did he rape her but he also passed her around from man to man. He was someone who otherwise was very influential and highly respected in his community. How horrific! I could feel her pain even as we prayed. Can you recover from such devastating issues? Yes, you can, by the grace of God. This woman had forgiven her father, but there was a wall she had built around her heart. It was as if I heard her say, "I have to protect myself. If I don't, who will?" She had made up her mind that she couldn't trust anyone, not even God. As we prayed, tears welled up in her eyes, and she decided in her heart, by the confession of her mouth, to let go of the distrust she had held on to and totally trust the Lord. The wall she had around her heart had kept others out. We prayed, and she confessed the lack of trust she felt. God miraculously tore down the walls of pain and distrust. If you can't trust God when you are living, how can you trust Him when you are dying?

People, family, and friends fail us, but God does not. He has the perfect plan. It's our job to understand what that plan is, what His will is, and then to trust God in it. Trusting God in the midst of such tremendous pain isn't an option; it's a must. That being said, there are many who have died gracefully, and it was the power of the Holy Spirit that helped them through it. We have to run our race to the very end.

> NUGGETS OF WISDOM: Therefore, since we have so great a cloud of witnesses surrounding us, let us also lay aside every encumbrance and the sin which so easily entangles us, and let us run with endurance the race that is set before us. (Hebrews 12:1)

Acceptance Through the Way

There comes a time in each individual's life where a decision is made. We must personally decide:

- Do I really believe in God?
- Is He real?
- Is there life after death?
- Is heaven real?
- Was there a man named Jesus who put off deity to put on humanity so that we could live, die, and be resurrected like Him?

How do you answer these questions? You simply choose to believe. Now if we die with Christ, we believe that we will also live with Him. We know that Christ, being raised from the dead, will never die again; death no longer has dominion over Him. When you become a believer, you are then united with Christ in His death, so that you will be united with Him in resurrection. Therefore, if we died with Christ, we will also live with Him. Death has no power over Jesus Christ because He was raised from the dead. We, too, as believers, will be raised to life as we go immediately to Jesus and will be given a glorified body at the rapture. Our spirit and soul will be reunited to live with Him into eternity at the very point of death. To be absent from the body is to be present with the Lord.

NUGGETS OF WISDOM: For if we have become united with Him in the likeness of His death, certainly we shall also be in the likeness of His resurrection, knowing this, that our old self was crucified with Him, in order that our body of sin might be done away with, so that we would no longer be slaves to sin; for he who has died is freed from sin. Now if we have died with Christ, we believe that we shall also live with Him, knowing that Christ, having been raised from the dead, is never to die again; death no longer is master over Him. For the death that He died, He died to sin once for all; but the life that He lives, He lives to God. (Romans 6:5-10)

Eternal life is promised through acceptance of the life, death, and resurrection of Jesus Christ. You see, it is because of a choice Jesus made. He chose to take upon Himself the sins of the world, to pay the penalty due to obtain the keys to hell and death for my sins and yours; and by this decision, we receive forgiveness for all of our sins: the resultant salvation and guaranteed eternal life, a glorified body resurrection from the dead. Therefore, we have been given the right to choose eternal life. The choice is yours today. It is in truth where you find your greatest treasures: the comfort in knowing that, no matter what, there is an afterlife. It makes acceptance possible.

SHAREWORTHY

Truth gives us the freedom to believe,
the willingness to hope, and the strength
to hold on.

—*Robin Bertram*

NUGGETS OF WISDOM: It is because of the Lord's loving-kindness that we are not destroyed for His loving-pity never ends. It is new every morning. He

is so very faithful. "The Lord is my share." says my
soul, "so I have hope in Him."
(Lamentations 3:22-24 NLV)

Acceptance Through Comfort

We can find comfort in such a time as this in the gospel. This good news should offer comfort to those who are facing darkness, tragedy, loss, long-term or terminal illness. Comfort is a valuable commodity when there has been so much pain. The Word of God promises the help of our Comforter, the Holy Spirit. We can take comfort in the reality of the Word of God. We can take comfort in the faith we have in God. We can take comfort in the hope we have in God. We can take comfort in the unfailing love of God. The Master and Creator of all things is our Comforter when we are facing life-altering situations: the loss of our health or even our life.

We also find comfort in maintaining normality as much as is physically possible. We can take comfort in the memories that we hold dear in our hearts. Remember the laughter. Remember words of encouragement. Remember every warm-hearted hug and the way your friends and family make you feel comfortable and loved. Remember the times of joy and celebration. We can choose not to forget the loving words and memories. These are the real treasures we have in life. There are no human words of wisdom to wash away the pain. There is no amount of knowledge gained that can release us from our sense of loss when facing these obstacles. There is no intellect that will reason through our grief. There is but one answer to the anguish we all are experiencing, and that is our hope in God alone. I have walked with numerous families who have suffered great tragedy or loss or had to suffer through long-term or terminal illness with their loved ones. There is no greater time to know Jesus than at this very time.

The great apostle Paul, quoting the Old Testament, put it this way: "Things which eye has not seen and ear has not heard, And *which* have not entered the heart of man, All that GOD has prepared for those who love Him" (1 Corinthians 2:9). Today you can choose to choose life. Choose eternal life in Jesus Christ. Say yes to His Word, yes to His truth, and yes to His love and His life. Choose to celebrate this life, knowing and taking comfort in the fact that there is a life yet to come.

We all leave this world. No one questions that. The question is where do we end up. We have only two destinations to choose from: heaven or hell. You cannot accept the reality of heaven without accepting the reality of hell. Hell is a real place absent of God, absent of light, love, or joy, absent of peace. It is a dark lake of fire for the eternally damned. Jesus said He is the way. Perhaps you're not sure of your destiny. You can be today. Pray this prayer with me.

> Dear God in Heaven,
>
> Thank You for life. Thank You for giving me the time that I have had. Thank You for giving me life eternal. Now Father, I ask that You help my heart not to hurt through this time. I ask for You to help me from being angry at You, others, or even the situation. I ask that You give me peace that passes understanding and comfort. I ask that You please help me to accept this reality. I cannot do it apart from You. Father, please do this for my family and friends also. In Jesus name I pray, amen.

SHAREWORTHY

Never be afraid to trust an unknown future to
a known God.

—*Corrie ten Boom*

Letting Go

You cannot change some things. There comes a time when
everyone in the family has to accept the inevitable. After sitting with
many who have gone home to be with the Lord, one thing is certain
to me: God prepares His children. It's as though they know and have
made peace in their hearts that their time has come. It is not uncommon for a loved one to hold on for dear life because they sense other
family members or loved ones cannot let them go. Herein lies the
difficulty. As much as you may love and care for the terminally ill, it
is unfair to hold them here because you cannot deal with them being
gone. It's important that they know that you will get by. They need
your reassurance that you will be fine.

Acceptance is based on the understanding that if we live, we live
for the Lord, or if we die, we die for the Lord. Therefore, whether we
live or die, we are the Lord's. We learn from Scripture that our spirit
returns to our Creator: "Then the dust will return to the earth as it was,
and the spirit will return to God who gave it" (Ecclesiastes 12:7).

A Divine Influence

Our greatest fears come from the fear of suffering, the fear of
loss, the fear of uncertainty, the fear of incompletion, and the fear of

being nonexistent. Suffering is a real concern. I understand that fear completely. I always say, "I don't want to suffer." But who does? No one wants to suffer. What I can tell you is that the dear ones I have walked with to their deathbeds made it through by the power of the Holy Spirit. There was a divine influence of the Lord right there, by their side, as they stood at heaven's gates. It was God, in the power of the Holy Spirit, giving them comfort. It was God strengthening them, comforting them, loving them. Yes, they suffered, but it was all very supernatural, and their peace was great. It was as though God was holding them in His arms. What you need to remember, regardless of your beliefs, is that you will exist: heaven or hell. You do not just disappear, fade away, or end; you will exist. You will continue on.

NUGGETS OF WISDOM: My body and my heart may grow weak, but God is the strength of my heart and all I need forever. (Psalm 73:26 NLV)

Unfinished Things

There is a real fear of leaving things unfinished. I struggled immensely with this in my own heart. I knew for years I was to write this book, but it sat on my computer halfway finished until I faced my own mortality. Then I knew for certain how important it was to finish the work I had started seven years earlier. You may not have that chance. You may have to leave things unfinished. You can pray and ask God to send someone to finish what you could not. Your work can be finished through your children and grandchildren. You can believe that God is in control and He knows what is best, and you can trust that if you need to finish something, He will empower you to do just that. His word promises: "For I am confident of this very thing, that He who began a good work in you will perfect it until the day of Christ Jesus" (Philippians 1:6). Take your work and give it all to God. He will watch over it, protect it, and finish it.

I also thought about my children and the birth of their children. I wanted to be a part of all of that. No one has any guarantees. For me, I thought about having my son and daughter carry on my legacy through my website, Bible studies, and writing. I knew that the most important thing on my agenda was seeing souls saved. I had to be okay with the fact that God did not need me; I needed Him. I needed to trust that what I could not accomplish, I would have to understand that it was okay. God already knew.

Travel Guide

Have I ever been to heaven? The answer is simply no. But I do not need to go to understand what heaven is really like. My husband and I love to travel. Before we go to a new place, we always buy a travel guide. It will include things like locations of interest, places to stay, where to eat, excursions, maps, exciting happenings, events, and activities. We go through the book and pick out all the places we want to be sure to visit. The guides give you a clear picture of the area before you ever get there. We rely on those guides because they are so incredibly accurate. Oftentimes they will give such great information, you feel as though you've been there when you actually do arrive. Wonderful resources. My friend, you have an incredible resource available to you: the Holy Bible. It is reliable, infallible, inerrant, and inspired. It is full of valuable information about our final destination. Take this time and understand what it is telling you.

> NUGGETS OF WISDOM: The last enemy that will be abolished is death. (1 Corinthians 15:26)

TREASURE CHEST

- Acceptance comes as we face the reality of life, death, heaven, and hell.

- Acceptance comes when we understand the process of dying.

- Acceptance comes when we understand that this is not the end but a new beginning.

- Acceptance comes when we understand that we will see our family and friends again.

- Acceptance comes when we understand that there will be a great cloud of witnesses to welcome us home.

- Acceptance comes when we understand that the things we do not finish were already know to God and what we needed to finish, He will make sure we do.

- Acceptance comes when we know that, without a doubt, God will be there and walk us to the gates of heaven.

I've a home prepared where the saints abide,
Just over in the glory land;
And I long to be by my Savior's side,
Just over in the glory land.
I am on my way to those mansions fair,
Just over in the glory land;
There to sing God's praise and His glory share,
Just over in the glory land.

—J. W. Acuff, *"Just Over in the Glory Land"*

CHAPTER 12

Everybody Wants to Go to Heaven, Nobody Wants to Die

"In My Father's house are many mansions; if it were not so,
I would have told you. I go to prepare a place for you."
—*John 14:2 NKJV*

My father used to sing a little song called "Just Build My Mansion on Hallelujah Street." I remember my mother fussing at him, "Paul, stop singing that song!" He would sit at the piano and sing with such joy. Daddy had been sick for many years, and his heart became greatly weakened and enlarged. It was difficult for him to even eat enough food to keep him going because his heart took up space that his stomach needed. Dad knew the time would soon come when he would leave this world. Although it reminded mother of the severity of the situation, my dad found comfort in those words. God has prepared a place in heaven for all of His children. There will be a glorious city, with all the saints that have gone before us, all of our loved ones who we held dear to our heart.

> NUGGETS OF WISDOM: But as it is, they desire a better country, that is, a heavenly one. Therefore God is not ashamed to be called their God; for He has prepared a city for them. (Hebrews 11:16)

Before any of us can enter heaven, we must leave our earthly body, our "houses of clay" (Job 4:19). We all, sinners and saints, face the end of association with this earthly body in which we are presently housed. Hope comes in knowing, however, that we do not fade away into obscurity. We immediately go on to be with Jesus, and we move into a higher realm of being. It's a promise we have as believers. Jesus said to the thief hanging by his side, "Today you shall be with Me in Paradise" (Luke 23:43). Not at some unknown future time but today.

The Reality of Heaven

Is there a real place called heaven? Can it possibly exist? Is it a place where there is real activity? All of these questions will find their answers when you first decide in your heart that you truly believe the Word of God in its entirety, nothing excluded. It is true and infallible—every word, every sentence, every precept, and every promise. Is heaven real? The answer is an unequivocal yes. So, what will heaven be like?

Inexpressible Beauty

Apostle Paul wrote that there was a man called up into paradise who saw things too inexpressible for words. Most agree that Paul had an experience that few ever get to experience. Most of us will never see heaven on this side, but we can still know for certain that it is real. Can you imagine a place so beautiful and lovely that you could not find the words adequate enough to even express what you were experiencing?

Twelve Pearl Gates and Foundations

What will we see? We will see twelve gates, with twelve stones on the foundation, with the name of the twelve apostles written on them. We will see twelve apostles, twenty-four elders, and four living creatures that are positioned around the throne of God. The gates are made of pearl. Think for just a moment. Have you ever held a string of pearls in your hand and felt the weight and smoothness? Have you compared them to the imitation pearls that you can pick up anywhere? As good as man is at imitating things, those imitation pearls cannot compare to the real thing. These gates will be beautiful, and those who accept Jesus will be permitted entry with open arms. We see from the Scriptures that there will be foundations adorned with jewels and precious stones. The foundation and walls will be magnificent, unlike anything we have ever experienced. There will be streets of gold and crystal seas.

> NUGGETS OF WISDOM: This is the message we have heard from Him and announce to you, that God is Light, and in Him there is no darkness at all.
> (1 John 1:5)

Light

Have you ever sat outside on a spring day when the air is still just a bit nippy and felt the warmth of the sun hitting your face? Do you remember a time at the beach on a windy day but the sun kept you warm and comfortable? In our frail and human thinking, we cannot possibly begin to understand the depths of the Scriptures that define heaven, but what we can do is differentiate in our minds the concepts of darkness and light. In darkness, it is hard if not impossible to see. In darkness, there is often a desire to find light. In heaven, we will not have to search for it. We will not even need sunlight because God is light, and His light will shine bright into eternity. The warmth of God's love radiates in our hearts, and the light of God pushes out the darkness. Heaven will be filled with glorious light.

NUGGETS OF WISDOM: And the city has no need of the sun or of the moon to shine on it, for the glory of God has illumined it, and its lamp is the Lamb. (Revelation 21:23)

No Tears, No Pain

Have you experienced great pain? We all recognize that pain and sorrow are a part of life that cannot be avoided. I think about the tears I have shed here on this earth, in this life. They have been many—sorrows too great to even share and deep pain that I thought I would never have to experience. My heart leaps when I read that in heaven there will be no more tears, sorrow, crying, or pain. This is a promise God has made to His people, and I know His Word is true.

He cannot lie. What joy, what peace, and what comfort we will experience when we get to heaven. The former things will be wiped away.

> NUGGETS OF WISDOM: And He will wipe away every tear from their eyes; and there will no longer be any death; there will no longer be any mourning, or crying, or pain; the first things have passed away. (Revelation 21:4)

No Marriage

For many, there is a concern regarding the question of marriage in heaven (see Matthew 22:30). Jesus taught that we will be like angels; therefore, there will be no marriages in heaven. However, we all experience great love; love will abound. If you've ever experienced the love of God in a real and personal way, then that is only just a taste of what we will experience in heaven. How can I say that with confidence? Because GOD IS LOVE. We will be in the presence of the very source and essence of love. What a joy! The love we will experience will be without limitation or skewed in any way. It will be unconditional. It will be boundless. It will be eternal. God is love, and through Him emanates the greatest love.

Jesus walked through walls. The natural realm had no effect on Him and presented no limitations to Him. He taught that we will be like angels (see Luke 20:36). Angels are powerful and free. They move without hindrance. We will not be angels; we will be *like* angels. The Bible actually reads that we will be above the angels and will actually judge them. In other words, we will not have the same limitations we have here on this earth but will have freedom we can only imagine. The things that have held us down in this world will not hold us down in heaven. We will be free, totally free.

No Hunger

Several years ago I led a mission trip to Nigeria. We were in a car being transported from the city to go into the village where we were staying. The driver asked if we might take a detour. He was a pastor of a little village church in the middle of nowhere. We arrived at his little cinderblock open-air church building and went inside with him. There were ten young boys who were starving to death. Their bellies were distended and there was no food available. I still remember the pain on their faces. These children knew real hunger. They knew what it meant to lay their head down at night wondering if they had enough food to sustain their life one more day. In heaven, there will be no more hunger.

> NUGGETS OF WISDOM: They will hunger no longer, nor thirst anymore; nor will the sun beat down on them, nor any heat. (Revelation 7:16)

A Wedding Feast

When we get to heaven, we will have feasts prepared for us. The Bible tells us that heaven is like a king who gave a wedding feast for his son. We celebrated our daughter, Taylor's, wedding several years ago. We served top-quality food and selected the best chef we could find in that area. The tables were adorned with gold glass chargers and gold flatware. Chandeliers hung from the clear ceiling, and the event overlooked the beautiful marsh in South Carolina. We wanted it to be so special for our little girl. It was tremendous.

In heaven we will enjoy delicious food. Jesus demonstrated this truth after His resurrection when He asked for and ate fish with His disciples. He did so to demonstrate to us what our resurrected bodies will be like. There will be plenty of great food to eat, lots of rest and enjoyment, and, most importantly, we will be present with our Father.

No Death

There will be no death in heaven. How glorious! We will be eternally connected to and in communion with our heavenly Father. We will not experience the second death at the time of judgment. We will live for eternity with our King. Death is about separation and loss. We are separated from our loved ones, and we lose the time we could have had with them. Heaven, however, is a place where we will never be separated from our spiritual family. We will never be separated from love. We will never be separated from those who have gone on before us. Heaven is abundant life.

SHAREWORTHY

Earthly work has earthly treasures. Spiritual work has spiritual treasures, which are reserved for heaven.

—*Robin Bertram*

Treasures Obtained on Our Journey

Heaven will house treasures that we obtained while here on our earthly journey. Yes, we will have a heavenly treasure chest of sorts. Why? Because the Bible tells us not to store up treasures here but to do so in heaven, where the moth and rust cannot destroy them. While here on earth, there are lives that we have touched, kind deeds or kind words with which we have encouraged others. Our treasures in heaven will be reflective of our deeds here on earth, and these treasures will never be destroyed, stolen, or lost. It's good to know that there have been things that we have experienced here that will carry on with us into our eternal home.

> NUGGETS OF WISDOM: "But store up for yourselves treasures in heaven, where neither moth nor rust destroys, and where thieves do not break in or steal." (Matthew 6:20)

Place of Joy

Heaven is a place where we will experience great joy because we will continually be in the presence of God. It will be greater joy than our best experiences here. Stop and think just a moment of some of your most precious memories. Those memories cannot compare to the joy we will experience when we get to heaven. God has prepared things for us that will be more glorious than we can imagine (see 1 Corinthians 2:9). It is promised in His Word. We will participate in great pleasures, and those pleasures will stem from being in His presence. Heaven will be filled with joy, singing, and celebrating our Savior (see Revelation 19:17).

NUGGETS OF WISDOM: You will show me the way of life. Being with You is to be full of joy. In Your right hand there is happiness forever.

(Psalm 16:11 NLV)

A Place of Worship

You might be wondering what we will be doing when we get to heaven. One of the most important things we will do is worship the Lord. We will be in awe of being in the presence of God, and we will then understand perfection and completion. We will enjoy, with great intensity, the privilege of worship. God is holy and worthy to be worshiped, so it will not be burdensome, but instead our time of worship will bring us great enjoyment also (see Revelation 15:4).

Have you even been out on a sunny day in early spring after a cold, dark winter and just thought you were in heaven? You look around at the new flowers as they are opening from the bud. You smell the fresh grass and feel a warm breeze blowing across your face. Life couldn't get any better. Perhaps not, but heaven can. Heaven will be better than your best day on earth, no question.

When people refer to heaven as being on earth, they are partially correct in that we can experience a personal relationship with God, and the benefits and joy associated with it, while we are still here. This is experiencing some of what is in store for those who will go to heaven when they die. However, not everyone will go, even those who call Him Lord but live as though He is not (see Matthew 7:21). There are so many misguided statements made in reference to heaven and hell. Have you ever heard this: "Hell will be just one big party and all my friends will be there"? The last part of that statement may be correct, but the first part certainly isn't. Just as heaven is a real place, so is hell, and I promise you it won't be just one big party.

Reality of Hell

Hell is described in Scripture as a bottomless pit reserved for the devil and his angels. It is a lake of fire where the wicked, all liars, those who perform abominations, and those who refuse to accept Jesus as Lord will be cast. It is a place of everlasting punishment forever separated from God. It's not a joy ride or a party, nor is it a place to cozy up to your friends. No, in actuality it is a place of shear misery, darkness, and torment devoid of love and light. The Bible says that it is a place of outer darkness where there will be gnashing of teeth and where the worms will never die. That may sound weird, but just imagine the utter black of the darkness night you've ever experienced and then multiply that exponentially in your mind.

What do I do to get in? No one in heaven will deserve to be there as a result of any merit of his or her own. Because of this fact, there will not be anyone boasting that he or she has earned the right to enter into heaven. The people who will live in heaven will be full of gratitude to God for being allowed to live in His presence eternally.

NUGGETS OF WISDOM: Nothing impure will ever enter it, nor will anyone who does what is shameful or deceitful, but only those whose names are written in the Lamb's book of life.

(Revelation 21:27 NIV)

Excluded from Heaven

In heaven there will be no unholy people because without holiness, no man will see God. So who will be excluded from heaven? Those who practice abominations will not be there. Notice the word *practice*. That is a clear indication of lifestyle. The list is long, but it is a list of those who refuse to change their lifestyle and continue in their rebellion against God. Let's let Scripture speak for itself (see Galatians 5:19-21).

Heavenly Kingdom

Heaven will be like a kingdom. There will be order and structure. There will be a hierarchy. The Gospel of Matthew is replete with descriptions of this kingdom. For our purposes here, we need to understand that God is a God of order, and heaven will also be a place of order, and not the disorder and disunity we so often have experienced here on this earth. In the Gospel of Matthew, we see that there are kingdom principles already set up that teach us how to live. The kingdom of heaven is like a treasure buried in a field.

> NUGGETS OF WISDOM: "The kingdom of heaven is like a treasure hidden in the field, which a man found and hid again; and from joy over it he goes and sells all that he has and buys that field."
>
> (Matthew 13:44)

We find hidden treasures in the Gospel of Matthew that give us a road map to kingdom living, kingdom principles, kingdom authority, kingdom power, kingdom character, kingdom mysteries, and the kingdom message. Often we wait until tragedy strikes to figure out how we are to really live. I know for me, I made major life changes. I want to live in service to the kingdom. I want to enjoy now all the benefits of kingdom living. I want to experience now the power of kingdom living. We really do not have to wait to find out what heaven is all about.

> NUGGETS OF WISDOM: Then those who feared the LORD spoke to one another, and the LORD gave attention and heard it, and a book of remembrance was written before Him for those who fear the LORD and who esteem His name. (Malachi 3:16)

Can you imagine? All of the conversations you've had about God throughout your lifetime will be recorded. I don't know about you, but that makes me want to shout His name, bless His name, share His name, and of course, pray in His name. Not only are our words in heaven, our prayers are there, too. God does care. He hears your prayers. He treasures your prayers. He acknowledges your prayers.

> NUGGETS OF WISDOM: When He had taken the book, the four living creatures and the twenty-four elders fell down before the Lamb, each one holding a harp and golden bowls full of incense, which are the prayers of the saints. (Revelation 5:8)

Ethan's Story

Can we look forward to the reality of heaven? My friend Ethan, as he was approaching the finality of his life, knew beyond a shadow of a doubt that he was going on to a better place. He would often tell others that he knew for sure that he would be with Jesus one day very soon and that he would be in heaven. Those were not just words he spoke. He was not just going along with the church catchphrase. No, when your life is coming to an end here, you get really honest about your faith, your true beliefs, and your God. Ethan was in his midthirties with four children under the age of twelve. He was a tall, handsome man with coal black, wavy hair, piercing blue eyes, and a beautifully captivating smile. He was solid, not stocky, just solid. At first glance you would never have known he was so sick.

I had been Ethan's prayer minister for several years while he fought his battle with a rare form of cancer. It was a tremendous honor. I went to many of his office visits while he received his treatments, and I spent time with his family. He became like family to me. Ethan was given a death sentence but decided to stand in faith for his divine healing. I would stand with him. I knew beyond a shadow of a doubt that God, at any moment, could heal him. It was time he would spend in prayer, in faith, and in spiritual growth, and I was privileged to walk with him through that process.

NUGGETS OF WISDOM: Yes, even if I walk through the valley of the shadow of death, I will not be afraid of anything, because You are with me. You have a walking stick with which to guide and one with which to help. These comfort me.

(Psalm 23:4 NLV)

When Ethan first received the diagnosis of his disease, he was determined that he would fight this battle, that he would do everything in his power to get better. In the beginning, he thought he could handle things. He soon found out that he could not, at least not on his own. We agreed to pray that God's will be done, a bold prayer considering the circumstances. Ethan would spend much time in prayer, in faith, and in spiritual growth, but it was not an easy road. I witnessed inner turmoil. I watched the gut-wrenching pain on his face week after week as the disease kept stealing from him his strength, his manhood, his family, and his life. Ethan was accustomed to taking care of things. He was bold, strong, competent, and fearless. During this time, however, he realized that his life and death were completely in the hands of God. He had made peace with the idea of leaving this world behind.

One day I received a call from Ethan asking if I would meet him at a gas station in between his home and mine. He said, "I have something I would like to give you." When I arrived, we stood outside of our vehicles, and he placed a CD in my hand. It was by a bluegrass group, a type of music that I really had no interest in. Rather puzzled at the gift, I asked, "What's this for?" "Jump in. I want you to hear it," he said. I went around to the passenger's seat and hopped in the front of his SUV. Ethan put the disc in the CD player and the song began to play. The song was entitled "Everybody Wants to Go to Heaven, but Nobody Wants to Die." We looked at each other and broke out into laughter. We laughed and laughed, and then we cried and cried—tears of peace, joy, and sorrow. I will never forget that night. I felt the presence of God like never before. Both Ethan and God taught me that night that death does not have to be feared, that it can graciously be embraced, and that there is hope available when there seems to be no reason for hope.

Even today that CD represents for me a dear treasure that was found at the gates of heaven. I would shortly be standing at the graveside of my dear friend. The tears rolled down my cheeks as the sound of the twenty-one-gun salute rang out across the hillside. But there was also a feeling of joy inside of me, knowing that my dear friend had made it home and that he was well prepared, at peace, and ready to go.

NUGGETS OF WISDOM: The death of His holy ones is of great worth in the eyes of the Lord.
(Psalm 116:15 NLV)

SHAREWORTHY

Fear is now faith. The unknown is now known.
The loss is truly gain. Heaven is your home.
—*Robin Bertram*

Choosing heaven means choosing to have a personal relationship with Jesus Christ. Such a relationship brings a foretaste of heaven to this life, along with an eternity of joy. You can make your decision today. Jesus promises that God has prepared a place for you.

I was in church one Sunday morning after my father had passed on to be with Jesus. It was several months after his funeral. I wasn't even thinking about my dad that morning, but I happened to glance up and, out of the blue, I had a vision. I saw my father in his favorite blue suit, with his warm smile and twinkling blue eyes, looking down at me. He was giggling like a child. I was standing at the gates of heaven. He was safe. He was happy. He was home.

God's plan is perfect and He will be sure to complete it.

God has prepared a place for you.

God is waiting with open arms.

> NUGGETS OF WISDOM: "Do not be afraid; I am the first and the last, and the living One; and I was dead, and behold, I am alive forevermore, and I have the keys of death and of Hades."
>
> (Revelation 1:17-18)

TREASURE CHEST

- God is light, and in Him there is no darkness.

- God is love, and there is no greater love.

- Pray about receiving a deeper understanding of heaven.

- Heaven is not an unknown to the believer; it is our final destination.

- Trust that God has the perfect plan for your life.

- Look for signs from God, and share those God-moments that you have experienced.

- Be certain of your salvation, and know that Jesus will guide you safely home.

LOVE IN ACTION

The Environment

1. Keep noise at a minimum.
2. Circulate fresh air.
3. Keep the temperature as stable as possible.
4. Bring fresh flowers into the room.
5. Ask whether the TV or radio should be on or off.
6. Ask whether the lights should be on, dimmed, or off.

The Visits

1. Call before you visit.
2. Schedule regular visits. Do not stay away.
3. Tell them after each visit that you will come again.
4. Plan to sit with your loved one and allow the caregiver a chance to leave for a break.
5. Be cognizant of the appropriate time for your visit to end.
6. Consider how your loved one is feeling that particular day and whether it is best to come back another day.

7. Encourage old friends from their past to visit.

8. Watch TV or listen to music together.

9. Offer to read the Bible to your loved one.

The Tasks

1. Rally a group of helpers that can help one day a week.

2. Run errands.

3. Help clean their home.

4. Care for the lawn.

5. Babysit or take care of their pets.

6. Go to the post office.

7. Drive them to their appointments.

8. Take them meals.

The Support

1. Assume your help is needed, offer it, and then do it.

2. Offer support through touch, hugs, and holding their hand.

3. Kiss them, hug them, or shake their hand when you leave.

4. Let them know you care and how you are feeling.

5. Help them get out as much as they can, if possible.

6. Take them to the beach to see the ocean.

7. Send cards, notes, old photos to them.

The Communication

1. Hold regular family meetings to keep everyone on the same page.

2. Call regularly, and return calls promptly.

3. Offer encouraging words.

4. Be conscientious of the appropriate volume level of your voice.

5. Be honest, but be gentle.

6. Focus on the positive and not the problem.

7. Do not speak as though they are not in the room.

8. Do not speak for your loved one.

9. Assume they can hear and understand even if they do not respond.

10. Don't use clichés, platitudes, or inappropriate jokes.

11. Keep your loved one's personal information private unless they have given you the okay to share. Do not assume.

The Things to Do

1. Ask them questions and do not minimize their concerns.

2. Help them make memory books, videos, recordings of things they want to pass down to their children.

3. Offer to help them organize items that they would like to pass down.

4. Make lunch or dinner for both your loved one and their caretaker.

5. Help out with the children by taking them to their regularly scheduled events.

6. Offer to take on small projects with your loved one.

The Prayer

1. Always ask how you should pray.

2. Understand that the way they want you to pray may change at some point, and be cognizant of that.

3. Ask before laying on hands.

4. Ask before bringing in others to pray with you.

5. Ask how often they would like you to come over for prayer.

6. Do not just assume they want you to pray.

7. Pray in faith, believing God can turn things around at any point in time.

Notes

4. Love Lifted Me

1. *The Nicene and Post-Nicene Fathers*, series 1, ed. Philip Schaff, vol. 7, *Ten Homilies on the First Epistle of John*, trans. H. Browne, ed. J. H. Myers (Peabody: Hendrickson, 1995), ninth homily.

5. Hope Floats

1. Steve Cooper, "A Place of Her Own," *Life:Beautiful* magazine, accessed March 15, 2018, http://lifebeautifulmagazine.com/departments/a-place-of-her-own.

2. Martin Luther King Jr., *In My Own Words* (New York: Hodder and Stoughton, 2002).

3. *Strong's Exhaustive Concordance of the Bible*, s.v. "elpis," Bible Hub, http://biblehub.com/str/greek/1680.htm.

4. *Strong's Concordance*, s.v. "elpis."

7. Fear Not

1. University of Minnesota, "Impact of Fear and Anxiety," Taking Charge website, accessed March 15, 2018, www.takingcharge.csh.umn.edu/enhance-your-wellbeing/security/facing-fear/impact-fear.

2. E. Stanley Jones, *Abundant Living: 364 Daily Devotions* (Nashville: Abingdon Press, 2014), week 13, Sunday.

9. Diamonds in the Rain

1. Gem Encyclopedia, "Tanzanite" Gemological Institute of America, https://www.gia.edu/tanzanite.

10. Pearl of Great Price

1. Earl Nightingale, "Acres of Diamonds" Nightingale Conant website, www.nightingale.com/articles/acres-of-diamonds/.

2. Michael Starr, "'Antiques' Most-Expensive Item Auction Flop," *New York Post* online, March 21, 2012, http://nypost.com/2012/03/21/antiques-most-expensive-item-auction-flop/.

3. "Famous Pearls," Pearl-Guide.com, www.pearl-guide.com/forum/content.php?103-Famous Pearls.

ABOUT THE AUTHOR

Author, seasoned conference speaker, and former host of the nationally syndicated television program *Freedom Today*, Robin Bertram brings a wealth of knowledge and experience to women's platforms across the country. Robin's passion for the Word, love for people, and heart to serve were developed early on in life as a "PK" (preacher's kid) and continued through her life's journey. She often appears as a keynote speaker at women's conferences, retreats, and media seminars, where her straightforward approach and in-depth biblical insight is healing hearts and transforming lives, as she delivers vibrant messages of encouragement, freedom, and victory in Jesus Christ.

Robin is vice president for Christian Women in Media Association, an organization dedicated to bringing spiritual and professional enrichment within the industry. She is also CEO of Bertram & Ross Consulting, which provides comprehensive training and services to assist and empower other kingdom professionals in the areas of social media, marketing, content generation, customer engagement, and business analysis.